YORK NOTES

General Editors: Professor A.N. Jeffares (*University of Stirling*) & Professor Suheil Bushrui (*American University of Beirut*)

Thomas Middleton

WOMEN BEWARE WOMEN

Notes by John Conaghan

BA (LONDON) MA (McMASTER)
Lecturer in English Studies,
University of Stirling

 **LONGMAN YORK PRESS**

YORK PRESS
Immeuble Esseily, Place Riad Solh, Beirut.

LONGMAN GROUP LIMITED
Longman House,
Burnt Mill,
Harlow,
Essex

© Librairie du Liban 1984

First published 1984
ISBN 0 582 79237 1
Printed in Hong Kong by
Wilture Printing Co Ltd.

Contents

Part 1

Introduction

The life of Thomas Middleton

Thomas Middleton was born in London in 1580. His father was a builder who had prospered sufficiently to leave, when he died in 1586, a competent estate to be divided between his wife and two children. Anne Middleton soon remarried. Her second husband, a thriftless adventurer, wrangled with her over the family inheritance. Over the years, according to legal records, there was a great deal of turbulence in the household, including, in 1598, violent quarrels between Anne Middleton and her son-in-law. The effect of these disturbances on the young Middleton can only be surmised.

At the age of eighteen he was enrolled as a student at Queen's College, Oxford. It is not known if he completed his studies and took his degree. In 1601 he is reported in London, 'accompanying the players', and in the same year he married. His career of writing for the stage began in earnest in 1602.

He was busy and productive from the first, collaborating freely with other dramatists, and prepared to meet the requirements of different companies. At various times he wrote for the Admiral's (later Prince Henry's) Men, the Earl of Worcester's Men, the Children's Companies, and the Lady Elizabeth's Men. Among his early plays, *A Trick to Catch the Old One* (approx. 1604–1607) shows what he could accomplish in realistic comedy of London life. *The Revenger's Tragedy* was played by the King's Men in 1606, and Middleton resumed his connection with this, the most distinguished company of the time, in 1611 with *The Second Maiden's Tragedy*. In 1624 the King's Men caused a sensation, and provoked official anger, with *A Game at Chess*, a satire by Middleton on the former Spanish ambassador, Count Gondomar. The author prudently went into hiding until the storm had blown over.

In 1613 he was commissioned to write and produce a pageant for the Lord Mayor of London, and succeeded well enough to be asked to do six more, the last in 1626. No doubt this work helped him to obtain the post of Chronologer to the City of London which he held from 1620 to his death in 1627.

The author of such powerful plays as *The Changeling* and *Women Beware Women* received no special critical commendation in his own lifetime. He enjoyed some success, but appears not to have considered his literary reputation, for he gave little attention to the printing of his plays. T.S. Eliot in his essay 'Thomas Middleton' writes of him thus:

> Of all the Elizabethan dramatists Middleton seems the most impersonal, the most indifferent to personal fame or perpetuity, the readiest, except Rowley, to accept collaboration. Also he is the most various. His greatest tragedies and his greatest comedies are as if written by two different men. Yet there seems no doubt that Middleton was both a great comic writer and a great tragic writer.*

Date and publication of *Women Beware Women*

We do not know when *Women Beware Women* was first performed, or by whom. The play was not printed until 1657, when the publisher Humphrey Moseley issued it, together with *More Dissemblers Besides Women*, in *Two New Playes by Thomas Middleton*. There is no mention of performance, apart from Nathaniel Richards's assertion, in the prefixed commendatory verses, that he had seen it 'Acted in state, presented to the life.' This is the only evidence we have that it had been presented on the stage up to that time. Attempts at dating by modern scholars have placed it as early as 1613 and as late as 1627. The year 1621, or thereabouts, seems to have the largest measure of acceptance. The masque in the final scene, including a descent by Juno, and observed by a numerous gathering in the balcony 'above', suggests a production at the Blackfriars theatre.

The Jacobean stage

The acting companies who strove to establish themselves in London during the reign of Elizabeth needed, among other things, luck and good management to be successful. They had creative talent in plenty, and no lack of audiences, but they had to contend with powerful opposition. Preachers and pamphleteers complained of profanity and immorality; the authorities of the City of London feared riotous disturbances, encouragements to idleness, and the spread of plague; the Privy Council was severe against anything it considered to be slanderous or seditious. Among the companies who overcame the obstacles and survived the vigorous competition which developed, the Chamberlain's Men, with whom Shakespeare was associated as an actor, writer and shareholder, prospered most. The building of the Globe theatre on the south bank of the Thames in 1599 gave them a lead over their then nearest rivals, the Admiral's Men. Their supremacy was confirmed

---

* *The Times Literary Supplement*, 30 June 1927, reprinted in *Selected Essays 1917–1932*, Faber & Faber, London, 1932.

when, soon after his accession to the throne in 1603, James I appointed them as his own players, and they became the King's Men. Thereafter, they were required to give performances at Court much more frequently than the other companies.

In 1608 they took occupancy of another theatre, located in the Blackfriars precinct, within the city walls and conveniently close to the busy area around St Paul's Cathedral. It had the advantage also of being indoors, so that the company had obtained what proved to be an excellent playhouse for winter use, while they continued to perform at the Globe in summer. The new premises had in fact been acquired for the company by James Burbage in 1596, but after he had gone to much expense to convert them into a theatre, he was prevented from putting on plays there as a result of a petition of Blackfriars' residents who anticipated that the peace and quiet of the neighbourhood would be disturbed. In 1600 the theatre was leased to the managers of a newly-formed company of boy players, the Children of the Chapel. These, and the Paul's Boys, were the 'little Eyases' whose popularity – so Rosencrantz tells Hamlet – threatened to carry all before it.* They initiated a distinction between 'public' and 'private' theatres, and inclined towards topical satire. When the Children ceased playing at the Blackfriars, the King's Men, seeing the possibilities, took back the lease, and were ready to give performances there late in 1609.

The new theatre (known to scholars as the Second Blackfriars, as there had been a theatre in the precinct in earlier years) occupied part of a large upper hall in the old monastic buildings. A space of 66 feet by 46 feet contained a stage, a tiring room at the back of the stage with an upper level, and an auditorium with galleries arranged in perhaps three tiers along the sides and back of the hall. The resources of the playing area included: doors at opposite sides of the back wall wide enough to allow passage to armies, processions, and properties; a wide aperture in the middle of the back wall, with curtains which could be opened to reveal the rear stage, either for interior scenes and 'discoveries', or to enlarge the main stage; an upper level (which accommodated the musicians as well as actors 'above') with windows, a balcony along its front edge, and an inward space; and 'the heavens', a room or hut situated aloft from which actors were lowered or raised, perhaps in a throne, upon an eagle, or amidst clouds, or thunder and lightning. There was no painted scenery. Inigo Jones (1573–1652) had been designing changeable scenery for masques at Court since 1605, but it was not to be used in commercial theatres until after the Restoration in 1660.

In their 'private' setting, the King's Men drew audiences of a different

---

* Eyases were unfledged hawks; hence the 'little Eyases' were the unfledged brood of young actors.

social constitution. Prices were higher: the cheapest seats cost six-pence, compared with a penny to stand in the yard at the Globe. Poorer workmen and apprentices would have found difficulty in affording frequent visits. Seats in the pit were twelve pence or eighteen pence, in the boxes two shillings and sixpence. A stool placed on the stage (favoured by gallants who wished to show off their wit or their finery before the rest of the audience) cost two shillings. In these circumstances, the audience could no longer be a representative cross-section of society. The distinction which was made at the time between 'gentle', discriminating audiences at the Blackfriars and vulgar, comparatively unsophisticated audiences at the public theatres is misleading in some respects. However, conduct at the Blackfriars seems to have been more decorous; audiences were more select; and the atmosphere would certainly have been more intimate, since the capacity of the theatre was probably well below one thousand, about one-third of that of the Globe.

All the theatres built in London after 1609 were private, apart from the Hope, which was built in 1614 for the dual purpose of plays and bull- and bear-baiting. Two of them, the Cockpit or Phoenix in Drury Lane (built in 1617) and the Salisbury Court (1629) prospered along with the Blackfriars. Of the public theatres, the Globe (rebuilt following a fire in 1613), the Fortune (1600; rebuilt in 1621) and the Red Bull (1605) flourished throughout James I's reign.

General background

From the fourteenth to the seventeenth century mercantile activity in Europe increased steadily, encouraged by new geographical discoveries and the example of the great commercial centres of northern Italy, Venice, Florence and Genoa. England shared in the general expansion, and as a result experienced far-reaching changes in its social structure. A prosperous middle class emerged, whose richest members could aspire to great eminence. Self-made men entered the ranks of the aristocracy, hastening the decline of feudal power. The numbers of people engaged in trade, from wealthy merchants to self-employed craftsmen, multiplied. The pace of economic development quickened in the reign of Elizabeth, stimulated by new manufacturing techniques, the availability of capital, and an influx of people into the towns from the countryside. In the early seventeenth century, the peaceful policies of James I ensured that trade continued to thrive.

London grew at a phenomenal rate. From the reign of Henry VIII to the year 1600 the population quadrupled, to more than 200,000, and continued to rise rapidly. The wealth and prestige of the city were a source of pride for the inhabitants, and of wonder to visitors. Entrepreneurs, tradesmen, retailers, labourers were drawn in from the rest of the kingdom, along with pleasure-seekers, people of fashion, and followers of the Court. The new social conditions bred a new consciousness, which the dramatists enlarged and made their own. They endeavoured to represent the diversity and deeper concerns of the scene of life before them, and succeeded triumphantly. For their contemporaries, 'all the world's a stage' was not an empty commonplace, but an image which they mingled with their serious reflections.

Social morality

For people of the Elizabethan and Jacobean age, the common good, the 'general weal', was a guiding moral principle. A self-interested outlook was strongly disapproved of. 'Wisdom for a man's self,' writes Lord Bacon in an essay, 'is, in many branches thereof, a depraved thing: it is the wisdom of rats, that will be sure to leave a house somewhat before it fall: it is the wisdom of the fox, that thrusts out the badger who digged and made room for him: it is the wisdom of crocodiles, that shed tears when they would devour.' * It was held that none should seek to profit at the expense of his neighbour, or look for more for himself than his place in society allowed. With new economic developments, however, came new opportunities for gain, changes in work-relationships and an increase in social mobility. Traditional ties were loosened and accustomed modes of behaviour came under strain. Moralists of the day reacted strenuously. To Christian condemnations of the pursuit of riches for their own sake were added demands for the regulation of trade and attacks on usury. While the importance of trade to the kingdom was recognised, there were deep fears about the effects on society of both the endeavours of many to accumulate wealth and the success of a few in doing so.

The view persisted that the old social order, with its clearly defined classes, gradations and callings, should be preserved. Anxiety about political stability and nostalgia for traditional forms of hospitality and neighbourliness inhered in this view; but it was prompted also by a concern for public morale. The old order assigned to everyone a fixed place in the scheme of things, and expected him to remain there. It gave everyone a definite social identity. In the certainties provided by that state of affairs lay a firm basis for trust in society. One aspect of their changing world which particularly alarmed people of the late sixteenth and early seventeenth centuries was the growing evidence of lack of openness, of men not serving the general good but concealing their purposes and pursuing their ends by stealthy means. The drama and popular literature are intensely preoccupied with deception in all its

* The essay is entitled 'Wisdom for a man's self'.

forms, from the cheats of impoverished rascals living by their wits to the intrigues of statesmen.

The sources of *Women Beware Women*

In Part II, *Novelle* 84 and 85 of his *Ducento Novelle*, published in Venice in 1609, a Venetian author, Celio Malespini (1531–1609) tells the story of the love-affair between Bianca Capello and Francesco de' Medici, second Grand Duke of Tuscany. This romantic account, which has its basis in historical events, is almost certainly Middleton's principal source for the main plot of *Women Beware Women*. It describes the elopement of Bianca, the daughter of wealthy and influential parents in Venice, with a poor young Florentine, Pietro Buonoventura; the hardships of their life in his father's house in Florence; the ardent courtship by which the Duke obtains her love; the favour which both she and Pietro enjoy at court; and Pietro's growing arrogance, which provokes the Duke into having him killed by the enemies he has recklessly made for himself. The Duke consoles Bianca and, after she has recovered from her grief, makes her his wife.

Other narratives continue the story beyond this point, as does a brief version by Fynes Moryson (1566–1630) in a section of his *Itinerary* which was not published with the rest in 1617 but which Middleton might have read in manuscript. They tell of a deep hostility between Bianca and the Duke's brother, the Cardinal. She attempts to poison him with food which she has prepared; but when he declines it, and the Duke eats it instead, she consumes some of the same and perishes with her husband.

Middleton changes the story in many significant respects for his own dramatic purposes. However, two features of his treatment of the source material are especially striking. First, he carries over the inconsistencies of Bianca's character. In the prose narratives, Bianca behaves as a dutiful daughter-in-law, is devoted to Pietro, and retains an affection for him even after she becomes the Duke's mistress. Yet, subsequently, she forms the malevolent scheme of poisoning the Cardinal. In the play, too, the callousness of which Bianca shows she is capable is disturbing. Her plot to kill the Cardinal during 'his times of frailty' (V.2.26) is notably vindictive. Second, Middleton insists on the opposition between good and evil, virtue and vice. The chivalrous dealings of Malespini's Duke, his courtly and patient wooing, are altered to an urgent seduction in the play. To make the sin worse, the union between Leantio and Bianca in the play is 'sealed from heaven by marriage' (I.1.45). In the narratives, the Cardinal is worldly, cruel and ambitious. Middleton's Cardinal is full of religious zeal and vehement against the sinfulness around him.

For the subplot, Middleton adapts a French story which appeared in 1597. An English translation, *The True History of the Tragicke Loves of Hipolito and Isabella Neapolitans*, was published in 1628. Parts of this source are followed closely, and the main plot and subplot are linked by incorporating the nun who assists Hipolito in the story into the character of Livia.

A note on the text

The octavo volume printed for Humphrey Moseley in 1657, containing the earliest edition of *Women Beware Women*, was carefully produced. The printing was accurate, and there is evidence of minute correction as the sheets went through the press. The orderliness of the text indicates that the copy which was used by the printer was a scribal transcription made for the purpose. Since the stage-directions do not reflect the practicalities of the theatre, it is unlikely that the first edition derives from a stage-manuscript. In general, the spelling and punctuation are so different from Middleton's that the possibility that the play was printed directly from a copy in his own hand also seems slight.

The edition used in the preparation of these Notes is that edited by J.R. Mulryne in the Revels Plays series, Methuen, London, 1975.

Part 2

Summaries
of WOMEN BEWARE WOMEN

A general summary

Livia, a wealthy Florentine lady, helps to bring about two disastrous love affairs which are the main concern of the play. She is an immoral schemer, an example to show women that they should 'beware women'. She assists the Duke of Florence to seduce Bianca, a beautiful young gentlewoman who has scarcely begun married life with Leantio, a factor or merchant's agent, living with his mother, a poor widow. Livia also arranges an illicit affair between her brother Hippolito and his niece, Isabella, who is being obliged against her wishes to marry the Ward, a young heir whose foolishness is manifest in every scene in which he appears. Livia herself falls in love with Leantio, who is desperate and bitter about Bianca's faithlessness. Matters come to a head when Hippolito, at the Duke's instigation, kills Leantio to preserve (as he thinks) his sister's honour; whereupon Livia makes public his affair with Isabella. And so enmities are inflamed, between Isabella and Hippolito on one side, and Livia and Guardiano, the Ward's uncle, on the other. Schemes of revenge are devised, which will take effect under cover of the masque which is to be performed at the wedding of the Duke and Bianca. This wedding is intended by the Duke to legitimise their relationship, after the Cardinal, the Duke's brother, has expressed the strongest moral disapproval. During the celebratory masque, Livia, Isabella, Hippolito and Guardiano met their deaths; and also the Duke, who drinks from a poisoned cup which Bianca had intended for the Cardinal. Bianca, striken with remorse, takes poison herself, and so puts an end to

Pride, greatness, honours, beauty, youth, ambition.

Of the main characters, only the Cardinal remains to point the moral and close the play.

Detailed summaries

Act I Scene 1

Leantio, who has been away for a while, is welcomed home very tenderly by his mother. He brings with him a beautiful young gentlewoman, Bianca, whom he secretly wooed in Venice and brought away without the consent of her wealthy parents. He assures his mother that they have been properly married, but she is troubled by her son's and her own lack of means to provide Bianca with the comforts she has been used to. Leantio fears that his mother's doubts might spoil Bianca's contentment, but his young wife declares that she will be well satisfied with a virtuous poverty. The two women withdraw, and Leantio expresses his sorrow that his work will take him away from his bride until the end of the week, and also his concern to keep her hidden, lest her beauty attract the young gallants of Florence.

NOTES AND GLOSSARY:

affection:	love
comfort:	gladness at Leantio's return
express:	'press out', draw forth
knavish:	rascally
unvalued'st purchase:	priceless acquisition
a white sheet:	shroud
mark:	something to take strict note of
conqueror ... content:	Alexander the Great (356–323 BC), who was said to have wept for lack of new countries to conquer
in compass:	within limits
theft ... withal:	'stealing Bianca away was a glorious crime, worthy of any great man'
sealed:	approved, validated
keep counsel:	keep this a secret
If ... check:	'if you are obedient enough to take notice of a reproof'
keep you single:	support you as a single (unmarried) man
not confined ... humours:	'not limiting themselves to what their social rank or merits can expect, but following their ambition and inclination'
spoil:	put off
commotion:	rebellion
when they're once up:	when they begin to dominate
a simple charge:	a considerable expense
courses:	behaviour, unworthy conduct
keep close:	stay indoors out of sight
to go ... ability:	to manage with what I can afford
swinge:	free inclination
take out:	copy
sampler:	a piece of embroidery
frame:	devise
bags:	money-bags
perfect:	blameless

nearness:	kinship, being a near relation
mend:	improve on
wants:	shortcomings
scurvy:	discourteous
defects:	deficiencies
successes:	fortunes in life
traffics:	trades
drinks of all fortunes:	experiences all kinds of good or bad things
turn up the glass:	turn over the hour-glass
my own care:	sense of personal responsibility
After the course of:	in the manner of
pride:	sexual longing
stick:	scruple

Act I Scene 2

The scene changes to Livia's house. She enters with two men who are staying with her, Guardiano and her brother Fabritio. A marriage is being arranged between Fabritio's daughter, Isabella, and Guardiano's wealthy young nephew, his ward for fifteen years. The discussion turns upon whether it is right to bestow a young girl upon a man whom she has not seen and may not like. Fabritio, a dull-witted man, sees no difficulty; but his shrewder sister perceives that women have the worst of the bargain in such matches. Isabella comes in with her uncle Hippolito. She is disposed to object to the marriage, on grounds of the Ward's weakmindedness. His extreme foolishness is demonstrated when he comes on stage with his man Sordido, conversing in a ridiculous manner. However, her father is determined that she shall marry him. Alone on stage with Hippolito, she notices that he too is miserable, and asks the reason. He confesses that he loves her, not as a near relation, but with a physical passion. She is taken aback by what she sees as a breach of trust, and leaves him.

NOTES AND GLOSSARY:

moral:	traditional, social
elect:	choose
tendered:	presented, offered
hanselled:	'foiled at the outset'; ironic – a hansel is an inaugural gift
meridian:	particular qualities
come as near you:	resemble you (as much as she could)
Counting:	considering
kickshaws:	trifling things
blown:	in full bloom

Then . . . parted: referring to the proverb 'a fool and his money are soon parted'

Light: set upon

stop upon't: consider it

joined . . . land: marriages between colonists setting out for America were often hastily arranged

walk out their sleeps: walk together during the time they should be sleeping

affinity: kinship

clean wrought: skilfully done

stranger things: between men and women not related

bushels: large quantities (of money)

trap-stick: also called a 'cat-stick'; used in a game in which a piece of wood is struck into the air

first hand: first strike

jacks: common fellows

beat: with a pun on beaten = embroidered

tippings; fair end: terms of the game

chimney-corner . . . hole: these lines are dense with sexual innuendo. 'Cat' was a name for a whore

fool: a dish of fruit and cream

sack posset: a hot drink made with sack (dry wine) and other ingredients

prone: susceptible to lust

a cock-horse straight: straight to a mistress

eggs-in-moonshine: poached eggs (eggs were considered an aphrodisiac)

took down . . . crow: bawdy terms for sexual arousal

liberty: limits of jurisdiction

merely: extremely, completely

set by: considered, regarded

cacklings . . . Capitol: geese were kept on Rome's Capitoline Hill

dwell here: 'dwell on' Hippolito's appearance

grace: a pun: Hippolito blushes 'gracefully'

You see . . . so: possibly this is addressed to the audience

condition: situation

portions: dowries, marriage-portions

lies in still: still remains a prisoner

four warring elements: the elements of earth, air, fire and water, which were believed to compose matter and to be competing for dominance in nature

arguments: topics of discussion

venture: what is risked or hazarded

come nearer: be more explicit

prevent:	anticipate, forestall
well fare it:	bid it farewell

Act I Scene 3

The next morning, Leantio is torn between his desire to stay with Bianca and the need to return to his work, which will take him away for another five days. His sense of prudence overcomes the pleasures of love and idleness. Bianca, who appears with his mother at an upstairs window, is unable to persuade him to stay with her and neglect his work; and the Mother chides her for trying to do so. After Leantio has gone, a solemn procession of churchmen and the chief nobility of Florence approaches. Bianca and the Mother stay at the window to see it pass, and afterwards Bianca suggests that the Duke looked up and saw them.

NOTES AND GLOSSARY:

revels:	merrymaking
smack:	taste
are said ... fingers' ends:	apparently proverbial, but the saying is not known. The meaning is clear, though: people are reluctant to resume work after a long holiday
and:	if
that:	his great 'care', diligence
Fondness ... affection:	doting is a foolish accompaniment to love
hot-cockles:	a game in which one player kneels with his eyes covered and guesses who strikes him
cracks:	is full to bursting
they:	people (in general)
respective for:	cares about
bore double:	carried two riders
which end goes forward:	what happens next
that disease:	improvidence
still:	always
dressing ... water:	using the reflection in a bowl of water to arrange her hair
State:	rulers, nobility
standing:	vantage point
gone down:	that is, from the balcony
blood:	birth
Against:	in time for
reverence:	solemnity
conceit:	notion, fancy
argument:	topic of discussion

Act II Scene 1

Hippolito has been telling his sister about his passion for Isabella. At first Livia reproaches him for falling in love with a near relation, but at length she gives him encouragement and promises to help him to obtain his niece. Isabella's arrival is announced, and Hippolito leaves. Livia draws Isabella into conversation about the Ward. They agree that he is a downright fool, and that to be obliged to marry him is an affliction. But then Livia declares that she knows a secret, entrusted to her by Isabella's mother on her death-bed, that would help to thwart the marriage, and Isabella implores her to reveal it. Livia tells a story of 'that famed Spaniard, Marquis of Coria': he, she says, was Isabella's real father. Consequently, Fabritio has no binding authority over her, and Hippolito is not a blood relation. To complete her cunning stratagem, Livia instructs Isabella to keep all this a secret, and when Hippolito re-enters, she withdraws, leaving them together. Isabella loses no time: she speaks enticingly to Hippolito, kisses him, reveals her intention of being unfaithful to the Ward, and departs, leaving him to wonder at this change in her.

NOTES AND GLOSSARY:

point:	an image of the compass-needle
blood:	kin, relations
unkindly:	unnatural
where . . . spare:	'where a great man's generosity brings him honour, it is mistaken economy to make sparing use of it'
free means:	abundant, available resources
change:	misfortune
reprehension:	reproof, reprimand
Thou . . . own:	'I cherish your life as dearly as my own'
perfect:	fulfilled, completely satisfied
I would . . . win:	'I wish your love were forfeit in the event of my winning'
lift:	jerk, throw, dislodgement
Find . . . me:	'when you have seen for yourself what I can do, praise me'
cordials:	refreshing medicines
forsworn:	decided to avoid
bless; you simple:	possibly addressing the servant as 'simple'; but some editors emend to 'bless you simply', that is, 'entirely'
Your absence:	'please absent yourself'
I . . . affect:	'When I give my love I do so very unreservedly'

That ... fault: too much liberality, over-generosity
towards: approaching, impending
a fool entailed: a fool by descent, a congenital fool
he halts downright in 't: he never advances beyond being a fool
age ... neighbour: age is beauty's spiteful neighbour
set by: put aside
once: ever
make shift: contrive, devise means
do you: may it do you
cheer: food, fare
that would start you: that which would startle you
mercy: divine mercy
odds: distance in relationship
fame: reputation
friend: lover
of a brittle people: 'as a frail race'
the great canopy: the sky, the heavens
marked: noticed
hope of second pity: hope of another act of friendship
sets an edge upon affection: makes desire sharper
housekeeper: housewife
cates: delicacies
Though you be one yourself: that is, a 'stranger', not related
What has she done: that is, Livia

Act II Scene 2

Guardiano enters with Livia, telling her the news about the beautiful young woman whom the Duke saw in the Mother's window and was much taken with. Livia sees another opportunity for her cunning, and forms a plan of assisting the Duke and so ingratiating herself. She sends for the Mother. Meanwhile, Fabritio enters, foolishly excited about the marriage between Isabella and the Ward, since Isabella has assured him that she loves her intended husband. With Guardiano he arranges for a meeting between the two young people on the following day, and leaves. The Ward and Sordido come in, engaged in conversation about the physical attributes a wife should have (which Sordido delivers in rhyme). After they have left, the Mother is brought in by Livia's servant. Livia makes much of her, complains that they have not seen enough of each other, and presses her to stay until evening for supper. The Mother is reluctant to stay; she explains that she has left Bianca alone; Livia insists that Bianca be sent for; a servant fetches her; Bianca is introduced to Guardiano, who offers to show her the rooms and pictures in the house while Livia and the mother play a game of chess. He leads her away, and the two of them reappear 'above', in another part of the house. Here the Duke appears, unseen at first by Bianca. Guardiano leaves, and thus Bianca is left alone with the Duke, who assails her virtue ardently. She resists at first, but he prevails with promises of wealth and honour. They leave together. Meanwhile 'below' on stage the game of chess parallels the action, Livia having outplayed the Mother. Guardiano enters and in an aside describes the trap that was laid for Bianca in the most cynical terms. Bianca now enters. She has bitter reproaches for Guardiano and Livia for their corrupt stratagems, but she conceals her mood from the Mother, and they go in to supper. Livia is unmoved, being entirely sceptical about Bianca's qualms.

NOTES AND GLOSSARY:

set forth:	describe
spied from:	seen looking from
Sunday-dinner . . . Thursday-supper:	perhaps the widow helped to prepare the meals
single:	coming from one person
too much worth:	extremely well rewarded
absolute:	perfect
court passage:	a game played with three dice
alteration . . . wisely:	sarcastic: for Fabritio to talk wisely would be an alteration
does he trow:	does he, I wonder
tricked up:	adorned, finely dressed
use:	custom
halter:	noose, an anagram of 'lather'
jiggam-bobs:	trinkets
After:	at the rate of
let his folly blood:	'letting' or draining blood was a medical treatment: Livia has identified Fabritio's foolishness accurately
world's end:	the absolute limit of foolishness
shuttle-cock . . . battledore:	equipment used in a game resembling modern badminton
ask . . . congregation:	a special licence was necessary if the banns of marriage were not 'asked' in church
pottage:	soup
plaguey guess:	colloquially, 'a very shrewd ability to judge'
pearl in eye:	having a white speck in the eye
ruby:	pimple
smack:	kiss heartily
hopper-rumped:	with large ungainly buttocks

ancient order:	referring to a passage in Sir Thomas More's (1478–1535) *Utopia* (1516) where naked viewing is recommended
for that trick:	being made to strip in turn
bum-roll:	cushion worn around the hips to hold out the skirt
farthingale:	a framework of hoops beneath the skirt
penthouse:	a sloping roof added on to a building (a shop with a penthouse over the window would be dark inside)
rotten stuff:	meaning venereal disease
take:	succeed, come off
tongue-discourse:	talkativeness
stroke:	stroke of the clock
friend:	lover
quean:	whore
sojourners:	guests
men:	chessmen
heat . . . part:	the time for your best exertions; your most taxing role
ability:	means, resources
'mends:	amends
humanity:	humaneness, natural kindness
motioned of:	suggested by
set us on:	incite us to quarrel
come off:	extricate ourselves
rook:	the chess piece otherwise known as the 'castle'
duke:	another name for the rook
hold:	wager
simplicity receives . . . one:	innocence is doubly afflicted
presently:	immediately
bold with:	unafraid of, hardened towards
fear:	frighten
Then . . . health:	'To be afraid of evil is my normal, healthy state'
wit:	good sense
merely:	completely
fetch you over:	get the better of you
blind mate:	checkmate which goes unnoticed
witty:	cynical, opportunist
queasy:	scrupulous
bit . . . appetite:	a morsel to sustain desire
Well advancement . . . endure all:	an obscure passage, perhaps meaning that the price of court-favour is high, but he is prepared to pay an even higher price
I pray . . . with you:	'You could say that of some of us also', that is, drawing towards the end of life

time:	age
in's kind:	according to his nature
blasting:	affliction by disease
Preserve that fair:	exculpate (Guardiano)
weight:	burden of guilt
How...make 'em so:	those who first make women into strumpets are even more wicked
wormwood water:	a bitter-tasting drink made from wormwood, a herb

---

Act III   Scene 1

The Mother, alone, reflects unhappily on a change which has taken place in her daughter-in-law's behaviour. She has become discontented and troublesome. Bianca enters, and immediately complains about the deficiencies of the house, which lacks the luxuries she is used to. They quarrel, the Mother reminding Bianca, in homely terms, that love and family life can flourish in poverty, Bianca claiming that her birth and upbringing entitle her to a better provision. After Bianca has left, the Mother compares this new attitude with her demureness when she first arrived.

NOTES AND GLOSSARY:

cutted:	abrupt, brusque
A grudging:	a slight symptom
takes:	catches
the new disease:	a fever which had recently made its appearance in England
cushion-cloth:	cushion covering
drawn work:	fabric ornamented by drawing out some of the threads
cut-work:	lace
casting-bottle:	bottle for sprinkling perfumes
to spare you for:	not ask you for
of duty:	as something due to her
offered under:	offered less
state:	wealth
orange tawney:	a fashionable, showy colour
white boys:	a term of endearment: 'lovely children'
she...bean-flour:	an example of wasteful extravagance
affect:	express itself
stoop:	bow
To the end:	with the intention
copy:	copyhold, legal tenure

quietness:	peace of mind
by her good will:	if she had her wish
pewter:	a metal in ordinary use, inferior to silver

Act III Scene 2

Note: In some editions Scenes 1 and 2 are not divided, but form one scene continuously. Scene 3, the banquet scene, is thence Scene 2.

Leantio enters, full of anticipation of the joys of wedlock after five days' absence. Bianca comes in with the Mother, and immediately spoils his mood: she wants a less secluded way of living, more opportunities of seeing young men, and less show of affection in their marriage. A messenger arrives and Leantio receives him alone. He comes from the Duke in search of Bianca, to invite her to a banquet at Livia's house; but Leantio convinces him that there has been a mistake, and he leaves. Leantio is now thoroughly alarmed. He wants to hide Bianca in a secret passage in the house, but she rejects this form of imprisonment with a show of indignation, and declares that she will accept the Duke's invitation. Surprisingly, the Mother is eager to attend the banquet too, and Leantio is left to meditate bitterly on

the fears, schemes, jealousies, costs and troubles,
And still renewed cares of a marriage bed.

The messenger returns: the Duke wishes Leantio to be present.

NOTES AND GLOSSARY:

Both at a twinkling:	both in the same instant
disliked:	displeased
tumbling cast:	fall, overthrow
another temper:	a different inclination
proneness:	disposition, eagerness
what's the humour:	what mood are you in
strange:	unloving
French curtsy:	French manner of greeting or compliment (with an allusion to venereal disease or 'the French disease')
fits him:	punishes him suitably
return the mistake:	take back news of the mistake
kept house close:	stayed indoors
court-green:	green on which bowls were played
mew me up:	imprison me
apprehension:	understanding
quickened . . . conceived:	with a pun on the sense of 'quick' = being with child
conveyance:	a secret passage

Kept in:	stayed indoors
trot:	change her gait (with a play on another meaning of 'trot' = old woman)
dry sucket:	a kind of crystallised fruit
colt in marchpane:	marzipan in the shape of a colt
knit to:	tied up in
perfection:	conclusion
you . . . too:	invent another mistake to protect yourself
used:	practised

Act III Scene 3

The scene changes to the banquet at Livia's house. Guardiano is preparing the Ward to meet his intended bride. The Duke, Bianca, Fabritio, Hippolito, Livia, the Mother and Isabella enter, followed by Leantio, who is filled with bitterness at the obvious familiarities between the Duke and Bianca. The Duke greets him with a show of cordiality and confers upon him the position of captain of the fort of Rouans. Leantio sees the purpose of this patronage clearly; and his misery deepens when the Duke proceeds publicly with his courtship of Bianca. Attention shifts to the marriage that is planned between the Ward and Isabella. Isabella is made to sing, to show her accomplishments, but when a dance is suggested, the Ward, whose foolishness has been apparent throughout, refuses awkwardly, and Hippolito takes his place. The inadequacy of the Ward gives rise to witty conversation between Bianca and the Duke, and they leave the banquet much pleased with each other. Meanwhile Livia has been observing Leantio and has fallen in love with him. When he and she are left alone on stage, she interrupts his tormented reflections to confirm that Bianca has indeed been unfaithful, and she offers him her own love, not forgetting to mention her wealth. After giving him time to overcome his grief, she leads him away to the prospect of riches and pleasure.

NOTES AND GLOSSARY:

express:	show, demonstrate
mark:	characteristics
deft:	dainty, neat
lusty:	large
sprig:	decorative piece of plant, spray
I'll . . . 'em:	it was sometimes argued that women did not possess souls
Rouans:	the name appears to be Middleton's invention, perhaps suggested by a place in Florence called 'le Ruinate'

bit:	morsel
stay:	defer (hunger)
means:	gain, advancement
sallet:	green vegetable, 'salad'
again:	as a result
goodness:	beneficience, favours
gilded bull:	that is, shaped in marzipan
plead your benefit:	claim exemption
Venus:	in astrology, Venus was a 'moist' star
With a full weight:	with all the severity it deserves
right:	rite
marriage tender:	betrothal
stirring:	excitement
parts:	accomplishments
wise-acres:	literally, 'pretenders to wisdom'; the Duke is being witty
ill bestead:	badly placed; in poor circumstances
a sweet breast:	a good singing voice (at line 157 Bianca gives 'breast' a plain meaning)
pricksong:	music sung from notes written or 'pricked'
baggage:	a playful term for a young woman
paint:	use cosmetics
to make physic work:	to help laxatives to take effect
compound with:	join with
keeps:	practises
blood:	feelings
a better order:	Hippolito has been first in her favours
fine-timbered:	well-built
fool me out:	deflect me from my purpose
office:	duty
prick and praise:	acclaim, high praise for her success
married man's dance:	alluding to the cuckold's horns
Plain men . . . minstrels:	listing various kinds of dance, associated with different types of people. Thus canaries refers to a lively dance, and a sweet wine, both from the Canary Islands
by attorney:	by proxy
glory:	show, ostentation
strikes by:	sets aside, dismisses from consideration
shift:	an attempt, an improvised endeavour
caroch:	a stately kind of coach
mistook:	wrongly inflicted
watched:	kept a watch
As if . . . for't:	as if we had been statues carved in a fixed embrace

close:	secretive
means:	addition of wealth, dowry
blow all fortunes:	come what may, whatever fate has in store
hearse:	wooden framework placed over the coffin in church
my factorship . . . with't:	my factorship is more remunerative
It suits . . . breeding:	'I have the courage, but not the training for the post'
Property:	nature (of the disease)
spare to speak:	refrain from asking

Act III Scene 4

Guardiano brings Isabella to the Ward, so that they can get to know each other better before the wedding which is to take place on the next day. The Ward, assisted by Sordido, proceeds to an unmannerly inspection of his wife-to-be, concentrating on her physical attributes, her face, kissing, teeth and movements. Isabella bears this without much resentment, since she knows that she will be able to deceive him as she pleases.

NOTES AND GLOSSARY:

contract:	marriage-contract
Like her . . . pays:	'the marriage will be physically gratifying (if you like her) and also financially rewarding (even if you don't like her)'
thrumming:	dithering, wasting time, 'twiddling'
shoot my bolt:	make my decision
birding:	bird-hunting; that is, courting
she-woodcock:	woodcocks were very easy to catch: 'a simpleton'
lost and cried:	proclaimed as lost by the town crier
eggs o' th' spit:	business to attend to
cater:	the buyer of provisions in a large household
nice professor:	precise, fastidious expert
verjuice:	the sour juice of the crab-apple (crabbed = sour-tempered)
comfit-maker:	confectioner
last:	shape (shoes were stretched into shape on a cobbler's 'last')
That's in . . . camp once:	a great deal of innuendo: buff was strong leather, worn by soldiers, whose camps are associated with venereal disease, which destroyed the bridge of the nose
bate her a tooth:	accept her with so much as one tooth missing
mannerly . . . handkerchief:	Isabella politely covers her mouth with her handkerchief when she yawns

goes:	walks
cleanly shift:	neat trick
scaffolds:	raised wooden platforms
upon ropes:	on the tightrope
simple:	extreme
breed ... teeth:	referring to the old belief that a husband suffered toothache during his wife's pregnancy

Act IV Scene 1

Bianca enters with two ladies. Conversation about their watches turns to talk about their lovers. When she is alone, Bianca reflects on her own sudden fall from virtue, and concludes that it is a mistake to bring up girls too strictly, since restraint increases the desire to live more freely. Leantio enters, and each is sarcastic about the other's new finery and wealth. His bitterness breaks out into abuse and threats, in the midst of which he cannot help boasting that his benefactress is Livia. He is appalled to find Bianca so hardened and shameless. She, while remaining outwardly cool and insolent, is secretly dismayed to hear about his friendship with Livia. He leaves as the Duke enters. Bianca reports this altercation to the Duke, and insists that Leantio is dangerous. The Duke reassures her and she retires to bed. He sends for Hippolito. As he expects, Hippolito, who has a fiery temper, is sensitive about his sister's honour, and is quickly roused against Leantio, especially when the Duke cleverly mentions that he had planned a noble alliance for Livia. Hippolito leaves, and the Cardinal enters. He is horrified by his brother's sinful affair with Bianca. In a vigorous sermon, he reminds the Duke of his responsibility for the example which he gives to his subjects. The Duke is seemingly moved, and promises to abstain from unlawful love. He forms a plan of making Bianca his wife – after her husband has been murdered.

NOTES AND GLOSSARY:

the sun:	a conventional image for the ruler: Bianca implies her relationship with the Duke
advocate:	possibly with the rarer meaning 'the secular defender or "patron" of a church or religious house' (*Oxford English Dictionary*, sense 4). The sexual innuendo is sustained in this dialogue
This ... me:	'the experience I have been through was the least likely thing to have happened to me'
jealous:	watchful
in sadness:	seriously
to see flesh stirring:	to see meat being sold (more generally: to see sensual appetites being indulged)

falls:	sins, lapses from virtue
simply:	absolutely, unquestionably
advanced:	raised in worldly prosperity
That:	that is, the window of her parental home
silk-worm:	wearer of silks, fashionable fop
ham:	the back of the leg
legs:	bows (with a bawdy pun)
want:	lack
service:	polite attention (also with a sexual meaning)
brave:	richly dressed
proud:	splendid
pass that:	go past that particular door
suckling:	child (of the devil, the 'great one')
breed teeth:	cut his first teeth
course . . . kennels:	a reference to the sport of coursing in which greyhounds pursue hares
When the moon hung so:	referring to the 'horns' of the moon and the cuckold's horns
with all forehead:	utterly shameless
monuments:	carved memorials to the dead
At . . . all:	at your most unseeing hour
Should . . . copy:	schoolboys learned penmanship by imitating the examples in a 'copy-book'
a blood soon stirred:	quick-tempered, fiery
goodness:	benefit, favour
that wind drives him:	the thought of his sister's gain will spur him on
ulcerous:	unsound, corrupted
poise:	weight, pressure
sped . . . of:	succeeded in obtaining
confessed:	made known
lost:	lost in thought (line 185); damned (line 186)
vengeance:	punishment
charged:	burdened
popular:	of the common people
example:	that is, giving a bad example
scattered parcels . . . bill:	separate items of a bill that has not been added up in total
such:	that is, great men
they:	great men
taken:	that is, by death
stay:	detain
this wall:	the perishable body
it:	lust
stoves:	heated room

Act IV Scene 2

The next morning Hippolito, now thoroughly angry, seeks out Leantio
and stabs him from behind. Leantio draws, but in the fight he is griev-
ously wounded, and he dies with bitter words against Bianca. Guardiano, Livia, Isabella and the Ward rush in. Hippolito tries to explain
his motives to Livia, but she, grief-stricken, turns on him and reveals
his affair with Isabella to the others. This discovery has the effect of
shaming the Ward, and putting him off the idea of marriage; it per-
suades Isabella to end her affair with her uncle; and it brings Guardiano and Livia together in a conspiracy of revenge against Hippolito.
The two of them conceal their malice and pretend a reconciliation with
Isabella and Hippolito. Isabella dissembles her goodwill in return.
Their attention turns to the forthcoming marriage between the Duke
and Bianca. Livia mentions a masque which was composed for the
Duke's first marriage, but never performed. They all take up the plan
of performing it on this occasion, with themselves as actors in it.

NOTES AND GLOSSARY:

blind time:	hours of darkness
apparent:	open
fear:	for fear
and:	if
Of a base stamp:	of a base kind (as a false impression stamped upon a coin)
mettle:	(1) temperament (2) metal
without voice:	silently, without warning
prodigy:	a grotesquely malformed shape
close:	secret
ignorant:	ignoring, inattentive
wore:	was given to, characterised by
graffing:	grafting
medlar-tree:	a tree whose fruit was eaten when ripened to a soft brown pulp (often compared with women of loose morals)
peep through a millstone:	proverbial for 'find out and resolve difficulties'
in the going:	while in motion
horns:	that is, cuckold's horns
pillowberes:	pillow-cases
hogshead of angels:	a large barrel of gold coins
scrivener's sandbox:	a box with a perforated top used for sprinkling sand in order to blot wet ink
one woman's murd'ring:	Livia has 'murdered' Isabella's honour

basilisks:	mythical reptiles whose glance was believed to be fatal
privilege:	immunity, protection
marriage-triumph:	the spectacular show put on for the wedding
time of hindrance:	period of disablement
approve:	prove
invention:	composition, piece of writing
pains:	trouble, effort
charge bestowed:	money spent
voice:	assent
make one:	take a part
The plot's full:	the cast is complete
state:	dignity
I weigh . . . have one:	'I don't mind, so long as I have a part'

Act IV Scene 3

The Duke and Bianca enter with the court in procession, all prepared for the wedding, The Cardinal enters in a rage, intending to stop the ceremony. He denounces the marriage as a sacrilege, a mere cover for sinful lust. The Duke insists that his motives are honest, and Bianca delivers an eloquent speech in which she presents herself as a converted sinner, the more in need of religion and Christian charity. They proceed.

NOTES AND GLOSSARY:

Hoboys:	oboes
her great master:	God
surfeit:	sickness as a result of excessive drinking
envy:	malice
He that taught you:	the Devil
read you over:	followed your meaning closely
can be sooner missed:	whose absence is sooner felt
professor:	one who professes religion
And will . . . be controlled:	'Lust will not be held in check until it is threatened with divine retribution'

Act V Scene 1

Guardiano tries to awaken some sense of resentment in the Ward, and instructs him in a method of revenge: during the performance of the masque, he is to open a trap-door when Guardiano gives the signal. Also, we learn, the arrows which the actors playing Cupids will shoot have been poisoned.

NOTES AND GLOSSARY:

galtrop:	caltrop, a spiked weapon used against cavalry
miss you:	that is, miss the signal
contumelious:	scornful
outparishes:	parishes outside the city boundaries
upon those:	that is, on the points of the galtrop
privy:	secret
mortar:	a strong container in which materials are crushed and powdered
present:	represent
to hit him:	that is, Hippolito

Act V Scene 2

The Duke and Bianca enter with the assembled court. He desires a reconciliation between Bianca and his brother. The Cardinal complies and kisses Bianca amicably; but she secretly still regards him as an enemy and has formed a plan of murdering him that same night. Indeed, the masque which is to be performed is full of deadly devices: the figure of Ganymede offers the Duke a cup which Bianca had intended for the Cardinal; Isabella, in the part of a nymph, offers poisoned incense to Juno, played by Livia; in reply, Juno 'throws flaming gold upon Isabella, who falls dead'; Guardiano gives the signal for the trapdoor to be opened, but falls through it himself; as Livia dies, the Cupids shoot their poisoned arrows at Hippolito, who, expiring, informs the bewildered company of the vengeance that is afoot. He hastens his own death by running onto a weapon held by a guard. One of the lords present gives the Duke a paper upon which Guardiano, before he died, wrote a confession of his villainy; but the poison which the Duke drank earlier takes its effect, and he dies. Bianca exclaims that the poison was meant for the Cardinal. Overwhelmed by a sense of her own sinfulness, she takes poison herself, and as she dies, remembers Leantio remorsefully. She denounces

> the deadly snares
> That women set for women, without pity
> Either to soul or honour.

The play closes with another pointed moral from the Cardinal:

> Two kings on one throne cannot sit together,
> But one must needs down, for his title's wrong;
> So where lust reigns, that prince cannot reign long.

NOTES AND GLOSSARY:

rid:	get rid of
model:	summary, abstract

event: outcome
abused: slighted, neglected
Hymen: the god of marriage
Ganymede: Jove's cup-bearer
Hebe: Jove's daughter
innocence . . . love: the Cardinal and the Duke
Via Lactea: the Milky Way (according to myth, formed when Hebe spilled milk from Jove's cup)
antemasque . . . entertain time: 'a preliminary piece to fill in the time'
in parts: each singer sings a 'part' in turn
design: indicate, nominate
keep true touch: behaves as it should
conceit: meaning, significance
tole: lure
quitted: repaid
forgetfulness: forgetfulness of virtue, moral obliviousness
a set match: a prearranged meeting: 'as if by appointment'
her fawning partner: Guardiano
reach: understand
springe: snare
him that fell first: Guardiano
Like: (line 214) compared with
remove: depart

Part 3

Commentary

A preliminary reading of the play

Act I

At first reading Scene 1 shows a domestic arrangement being agreed upon. Leantio's young bride is happy to adapt to her new circumstances; his mother, after some hesitation, is welcoming; and he is delighted with his good fortune. But already doubts are entering our minds. Bianca has 'forsook friends, fortunes and my country' (line 131) to marry Leantio. She is young, inexperienced, in a strange land. Leantio's feelings of love are mixed with other sensations: self-congratulation, sensuality, acquisitiveness and possessiveness. Bianca is a 'purchase', a 'treasure', a 'jewel', something to be carefully and cunningly hidden from the eyes of the world.

Scene 2 gives us a contrast. Instead of an imprudent love-match, we have negotiations for a marriage which takes no account of the feelings or suitability of the two young people. It is a worldly transaction, conducted by a parent and a guardian. Livia has a good deal to say about the wrongs inflicted on young women by such objectionable matches. Indeed, we see the evils of Isabella's situation, in that her father's stubbornness exposes her to her uncle's dangerous physical passion. In this scene we observe a society in which opportunism and worldly interest prevail, and in which there is no stability of moral values.

In Scene 3, the social differences which will be so fateful in the play are set before us. First, there is a sentimental leave-taking between Leantio and Bianca, with homely advice from the Mother. The circumstances are typical of an ordinary, thrifty way of life: Leantio has to go to work to earn a meagre living. Then the Duke enters in a grand procession. Bianca is obviously impressed.

Act II

Livia's evil influence expands, becomes a force in the play. She appears to be without conscience or sense of honour:

> 'tis but a hazarding
> Of grace and virtue, and I can bring forth
> As pleasant fruits as sensuality wishes,
> In all her teeming longings.
>
> (II.1.29–32)

She takes a pride in her skill in bringing about the downfall of chastity. The elaborate lies which she tells Isabella show how cleverly she has assessed the young girl's state of mind: her desperation at being forced to marry a man she despises, and the feelings of friendship which she already has for her uncle. Hippolito, for his part, is wholly abandoned to physical desire. Like him, perhaps, we are surprised by the sudden change which takes place in Isabella's behaviour, and the readiness with which she herself adopts a cynical attitude. It prepares us somewhat for Bianca's swift downfall.

Scene 2 is momentous, an impressive display of dramatic power. At first, Guardiano and Fabritio, then the Ward and Sordido, set the tone. Everything about these characters is base, or witless, or both. Serious matters are trivialised, and any sense of higher values is banished. Then the action proceeds smoothly and remorselessly. Livia's plot unfolds: Bianca is delivered into the clutches of the Duke 'above' in a carefully planned series of moves, while the game of chess continues below on stage. The boldness of Middleton's stagecraft forces us to be objective. We react with horror, but also with a clear awareness of the facts. Our sense of violated faith, honour and morality is not softened by pity or sympathy.

Act III

The harsh ironies of the new situation bear down heavily upon Leantio. His first speech on entering is full of praise for the joys of 'honest wedlock'. He ends the scene, having been deserted by Bianca, cursing marriage as 'the ripe time of man's misery'. All his opinions have been reversed. From comparing his situation complacently with the perils of 'base lust', he falls to envy of the loose-living, carefree, single man. It is ironic, too, that Bianca's attitude fulfils the worst fears of the Mother and Leantio in the first scene of the play. Now, she claims a 'maintenance fitting her birth' (though it can hardly be said 'her virtues': I.1.66), and she intends to follow 'the licentious swinge of her own will' (I.1.92).

Scene 3* mingles all the love-matters in the play. Bianca and the Duke, Leantio, the Ward, Isabella and Hippolito are all present, in their various involvements; and in this scene Livia notices and then falls in love with Leantio. It is remarkable evidence of Middleton's skill that he can deal with all these different concerns n the same scene. The banquet is the convivial setting for a lurid mixture of impudence, lust, bitterness, deceit and folly. The circumstances work upon Leantio's feelings and raise them to a high level of intensity. For the first time, we are given a romantic account of his wooing of Bianca (lines 252–62):

* Scene 2 in some editions.

> Canst thou forget
> The dear pains my love took? How it has watched
> Whole night together, in all weathers for thee...

But straight away, as if to show the shallowness of his nature even in this extremity, he falls prey to Livia and her promises of wealth.

Scene 4 is light relief in one sense; but it also shows the institution of marriage in a wretched light. It is a market in which people, in Isabella's words, are 'bought and sold' (line 36). Everywhere in the play, love is overwhelmed by selfishness and greed.

Act IV

Henceforward there is little occasion for levity. The play becomes more sombre, the atmosphere heavy with moral reproach and malevolent plotting. Leantio's invective against Bianca does not convince us of his righteousness. He wears the finery provided by Livia: he seems to be striking a pose even while he gives vent to his bitterness. Bianca, now very hardened, dismisses him as 'a poor base start-up':

> Life! because has got
> Fair clothes by foul means, comes to rail, and show 'em.
> (IV.1.110−11)

But the Cardinal's exhortations to the Duke carry more weight. We see him for the first time in this scene, and he has an immediate impact on the play. He provides a firmly fixed moral and religious viewpoint, in contrast to the ineffective, confused and erratic morality of the rest.

Leantio's death in Scene 2 has only a subdued effect on our emotions. The duel with Hippolito is a sordid scuffle. Neither man has any claims to virtue or integrity; and Livia's 'honour' is a hollow pretext. But Livia's attachment to Leantio is deep: crucially, since her grief causes her to make disastrous revelations about Hippolito and Isabella. Isabella's reaction resembles Bianca's in Act II, Scene 2: she has sinned, but she hates the person who committed the doubly dangerous sin of deceiving her into wickedness.

Bianca's speech to the Cardinal in Scene 3 is remarkable both for its cool impudence and for its smooth reasoning. She is almost plausible, covering her sin with specious arguments. Vice has now advanced to a spectacular eminence: to seduction and murder is to be added sacrilegious misuse of matrimony.

Act V

The downfall of wickedness is equally, and appropriately, spectacular. The pompous nuptials for Bianca and the Duke, which are based upon the ruins of a marriage which began in humble circumstances, end in death and disaster. The celebratory masque becomes a cover for murderous plots which make a mockery of its showy grandeur. Hippolito's last speech sums up the evil-doing and the retribution which has overtaken them all:

> Lust and forgetfulness has been amongst us,
> And we are brought to nothing.

(V.2.146)

Characters

Some of the characters can be easily understood by their obvious qualities: the Ward's foolishness, Guardiano's cynical worldliness, the Cardinal's righteous zeal, and so on. Others are more difficult to comprehend. Sometimes (it seems) they are inconsistent. Middleton is fond of showing rapid changes in the thinking and conduct of his characters, reflecting the instability and inconstancy of human nature. The more complex of the characters are described here.

Leantio

At the beginning of the play Leantio describes himself as 'knavish', and the suggestion that he is something of a rascal, a scapegrace overindulged by his mother, is confirmed by his account of the 'theft' of Bianca from her parents (I.1.37–50). From his description, it strikes us as an escapade – risky, but with a lucky outcome for him. His feelings towards Bianca do not seem to be romantic: rather, he is elated by his good fortune, and especially glad that his sexual appetite will be satisfied, and that he will not have to resort to loose company (I.1.26–34). The need for secrecy, for fear of Bianca's parents, suits his purpose. He wants to keep Bianca in seclusion, away from the eyes of other men; and he has no scruples about using his mother as a watchful guard (I.l.175 – 6).

His social position is humble in comparison with the company he will keep as the play proceeds. He has no means other than his factorship, which, as his mother says, will hardly support him as a single man (I.1.63–4). The difference in social status between himself and Bianca makes him vulnerable. Bianca, coming from a wealthy background, would normally have married a wealthier man. The Duke gets to know the circumstances, and makes much use of Bianca's unaccustomed poverty in order to obtain her (II.2.375–86).

Leantio is utterly baffled and dejected when Bianca deserts him. He appears not to have sufficient inner resources to sustain him in his plight:

> I'm like a thing that never was yet heard of,
> Half merry and half mad . . .
>
> (III.3.52–3)

There is something shallow and facile in his character. He is insecure, out of his depth. His death lacks tragic dimensions. On the other hand, Livia falls genuinely in love with him. Her words over his dead body hint at a spirited, athletic quality, a kind of vitality:

> . . . this sad burden, who in life wore actions,
> Flames were not nimbler.
>
> (IV.2.90–1)

The Mother

At sixty, Leantio's mother is a 'poor old widow' (IV.1.164), an unpretentious woman who lacks the strength or ability to impose her will on others. She quickly gives in to her son when he brings Bianca into her home; she is easily manipulated by Livia; and she is soon dominated by Bianca when the younger woman changes her manner and becomes demanding. Her last appearance is at the banquet in Act III, Scene 3. Thereafter she disappears from view (she is not present, notably, to mourn the death of her son). But still, she makes a lasting impression. Her practical, homely advice to Leantio in Act I, Scene 1; her remonstrations with Bianca in Act I, Scene 3, and her sharper retort at III.1.31, convey ordinary domestic values and housewifely concerns in a realistic way. Her decision to accompany Bianca to the banquet against Leantio's wishes is therefore all the more disturbing. Bianca interprets her motives in the most cynical way:

> Why here's an old wench would trot into a bawd now,
> For some dry sucket, or a colt in marchpane.
>
> (III.2.188–9)

Her conversation with Livia over the game of chess in Act II, Scene 2 is full of ambiguities which may or may not be intentional. Is she really an innocent, we are bound to wonder, or does she have worldly-wise suspicions about what is going on?

Bianca

The alteration in Bianca, from the demure, amenable young wife in Act I, Scene 1 to the treacherous, hardened court-mistress of subsequent scenes, is one of the difficulties of the play. Is her character consistent enough to be credible? Are there 'two Biancas'? Has the dramatist neglected to provide an understandable continuity in her transition from one form of behaviour to another? Perhaps the answer to these questions is to be found in Bianca's account of her childhood disposition in Act III, Scene 1, lines 52–9:

> I ask less now
> Than what I had at home when I was a maid,
> And at my father's house; kept short of that
> Which a wife knows she must have, nay, and will,
> Will, mother, if she be not a fool born;
> And report went of me that I could wrangle
> For what I wanted when I was two hours old;
> And by that copy, this land still I hold.

Bianca is naturally determined and self-willed. The modesty of her first speech is no more a guide to her real nature than her plausible self-defence to the Cardinal in Act IV, Scene 3. She has 'wit', in the dubious sense in which the word is used in the play. She is quick to see where her advantage lies, alert to seize her opportunities, and skilled in the use of clever arguments. Towards Leantio and, later, the Cardinal, she shows herself to be vindictive and without conscience. But she is capable of moral reflection, as in Act IV, Scene 1, where she considers the dangers that befall young girls (lines 23–40), and at her death, when she is painfully aware of the 'breach of marriage'. To an extent, she is the victim of Livia's ruthless and cunning plot; but it seems that her nature is very apt for depravity.

Livia

Our first impressions of Livia are of cleverness, worldliness, 'sophistication'. Hippolito and Isabella look to her for advice. With Hippolito, she is shameless and immoral. With Isabella, who is young and virtuous, she is deeply cunning, first gaining her confidence, then constructing a story to mislead her. She reveals a formidable knowledge of the weaknesses of human nature, and has evidently already had considerable practice in intrigue:

> Sir, I could give as shrewd a lift to chastity
> As any she that wears a tongue in Florence.

(II.1.36–7)

Mature in years, twice widowed, wealthy and with a high social position, she finds that her experience, abilities and quick intuition equip her for a dominant role. The quality which enlarges her further is her capacity for passion. She describes herself as being loving in the extreme, at the expense of her own honour (II.1.63–73). Certainly, the manner in which she falls in love with Leantio is spontaneous and unreserved:

LIVIA: Is that your son, widow?
MOTHER: Yes, did your ladyship
          Never know that till now?
LIVIA: No, trust me, did I.
          [Aside] Nor ever truly felt the power of love
          And pity to a man, till now I knew him.
                                    (III.3.59–62)

She is deeply affected by his death, and afterwards employs her subtlety in schemes of revenge. At her death, she expresses no remorse for her ruthless plots against the virtue of Bianca and Isabella. In her own mind, her sin was 'ambition' (V.2.133). From the beginning her conscience has been hardened and insensitive in matters of sexual morality, and her circumstances are such that her scope for evil-doing is unrestricted.

Hippolito

Until he kills Leantio, Hippolito appears to be a weak-willed, purposeless character, languishing on account of his love for his niece. Like most of the other characters, he lacks principles, and he conveys the nullity of moral values in the play by his very passivity. He complies unresistingly with the evil promptings of Livia and the Duke. He has some good nature, but little control over his own unworthy impulses. The Duke knows that beneath his apparent torpor there is a volatile temperament:

He is a blood soon stirred, and as he's quick
To apprehend a wrong, he's bold and sudden
In bringing forth a ruin.

                                    (IV.1.131–3)

In an impressive dying speech, he reviews the course of evil in the play (V.2.146–66). At this point he is repentant and clearsighted. We may conclude that he had potential for good, but that the better side of his nature was never properly developed. He has lived in a world where, it seemed, 'one must be vicious' (IV.2.4).

Isabella

Events in the main plot draw attention away from the plight of Isabella; but her situation is desperate indeed, and the ridiculousness of the Ward does not, or should not, dull our response to the intensity of her feelings. It is she who expresses the most idealistic view of marriage in the play:

> Yet honesty and love makes all this happy,
> And, next to Angels', the most blest estate.
>
> (I.2.177–8)

Her father's stupid and inflexible intention of marrying her to the Ward leaves her no way of escape except through duplicity and infidelity. Once Livia has deceived her with a false story about her parentage, her virtuous resistance to Hippolito collapses. Like Hippolito (II.1.228–38) we may wonder at the change which comes over her. Have we witnessed a deep transformation, an instance of a pure girl being deliberately and easily corrupted; or was her virtue not really very secure, her nature weak and inclined to concupiscence? There is a similar ambiguity in her rejection of her affair with Hippolito (IV.2.129–50). Her religious fears do not consist with her intention of seeking revenge. Goodness is destroyed in her with startling rapidity. The Cardinal's words in his final speech are particularly applicable to her:

> Sin, what thou art these ruins show too piteously.
>
> (V.2.222)

The Duke

The Duke first comes to our attention in the procession in Act I, Scene 3. We learn from the Mother that he is fifty-five (line 91) and burdened with the cares of state (lines 106–11). Quite a different impression of his character is given by the conversation between Guardiano and Livia in Act II, Scene 2. He is amorously inclined, and, in the case of Bianca, infatuated (lines 15–18). In persuading Bianca (lines 317–87) he reveals a knowledge of human weaknesses, mingling veiled threats with inducements of wealth and 'honour'. He is subtle in the use of power, expert in exploiting the selfish desires of those he rules. Livia and Guardiano hasten to deliver Bianca into his arms; Leantio is deftly removed by cleverly inciting Hippolito to kill him (IV.1.142–59). There is no opposition to him apart from his brother, the Cardinal, who is, for a time, taken in by his hypocrisy (IV.1.259–62). In the course of the play, evidence accumulates to suggest that he is indeed responsible, at least in part, for the spread of moral corruption in Florence. His urbanity and amiability disguise a ruthless, dissolute nature.

Structure

In general terms, *Women Beware Women* comprises two plots and two phases of action.

The main plot concerns Bianca's desertion of Leantio for the Duke. A second plot has Isabella seeking refuge from a distasteful marriage in a love-affair with her uncle. Livia participates in both plots, and so draws them closer together; and it is her involvement with Leantio which leads to the fatal duel with Hippolito and thence to the slaughter of the final scene. In the design of the play she is central.

Between the main plot and the secondary plot there are obvious parallels and similarities which help to concentrate and amplify the meaning of the play. Like Bianca, Isabella is deceived and drawn into ways of depravity by Livia's scheming. The downfall of both young women is swift, as if something in their own natures prompted them, but both feel a grievous hatred for the person who misled them (in Bianca's case, Guardiano as well as Livia: II.2.420−44). Isabella is corrupted first, so we are fully aware of the danger that Bianca is in when she is brought to Livia's house. In places where the two plots interconnect, interest is particularly intense. Thus, when Bianca is 'witty' on the subject of Isabella's future husband (III.3.230−5) we reflect on her own situation, and wonder how she thinks of Leantio.

The first phase of the action culminates in the banquet in Act III, Scene 3. All the important characters except the Cardinal are present. The setting is rich and splendid, the atmosphere fraught with emotion. In this scene Bianca's treachery, the 'breach' of the bond of marriage, is finally accomplished. Leantio has to bring himself to face the facts:

LIVIA: Then first, sir,
To make away all your good thoughts at once of her,
Know most assuredly she is a strumpet.
LEANTIO: Ha? most assuredly! Speak not a thing
So vile so certainly, leave it more doubtful.
(lines 273−7)

Leantio's mother makes her last appearance in this scene. She speaks only once, and has no further part in the action.

The final scene of Act III, in which the Ward and Sordido inspect Isabella, slows the action somewhat. Act IV begins quietly, with jocular conversation between Bianca and two ladies. But then Leantio enters, the play resumes its intensity, and the second phase begins. The Cardinal's uncompromising religious and moral views add another dimension to the play. The confusion of values which has arisen in the absence of any fixed moral standards is cleared away. In the dire events which follow we can see a pattern of retribution, of wickedness being punished as it deserves.

Morality

In his prefatory verses to the first printing of *Women Beware Women*, Nathaniel Richards stressed one aspect of its morality:

> Drabs of state vexed
> Have plots, poisons, mischiefs that seldom miss
> To murder virtue with a venom kiss.

It is certainly true that the vindictiveness shown by women in the play – Livia, Bianca and Isabella – makes a strong impression. In the case of Livia, we are made aware from the first that she has no sense of virtue. Her wickedness is in character, and so is somewhat less shocking than the degeneracy shown by Bianca and Isabella after they have succumbed to temptation. In the course of the play, a close association develops between sexual depravity and prompt, cruel vengefulness. Thus Isabella expresses her hatred for Livia:

> But for her,
> That durst so dally with a sin so dangerous,
> And lay a snare so spitefully for my youth,
> If the least means but favour my revenge,
> That I may practise the like cruel cunning
> Upon her life, as she has upon mine honour,
> I'll act it without pity.
>
> (IV.2.144–50)

Bianca's ruthlessness in dealing with Leantio, and in attempting to murder the Cardinal, is startling. We are not entirely prepared for her sudden extremes of malevolence.

In his dying speech in the final scene Hippolito describes what has taken place:

> Lust and forgetfulness has been amongst us,
> And we are brought to nothing.
>
> (V.2.146–7)

'Forgetfulness' is striking: it indicates that the primary cause of their downfall is not desperate, hardened criminality, but a wilful obliviousness to the demands of virtue and right principles. The main characters cannot be said to be lacking in moral awareness. They *know* what is right. Several of them are remarkably reflective. In speech after speech, moral questions are analysed and considered. Leantio welcomes marriage as a preservative from loose living (I.1.12–38); Livia discusses the wrongs of forced marriages and the position of women (I.2.29–45); Bianca is thoughtful about the upbringing of girls (IV.1.23–40). The Duke cannot be said to be given to moral deliberations, but he has the Cardinal to remind him, in two powerful tirades, in Act IV, Scenes 1 and 3.

The combination of moral awareness and evil intent produces some corrupt inconsistencies. Hippolito makes a distinction between concealed and open sinning (IV.2.1–10); Isabella's vow of vengeance against Livia (above) is preceded by remorse for her fall from virtue; the Duke plans to remove the scandal from his relationship with Bianca – and murder her husband (IV.1.267–78). In Act IV, Scene 2, in the feigned reconciliation between Livia and Guardiano and Hippolito and Isabella, the language of virtue cloaks the most villainous designs. Standards of good are acknowledged – and casually and cynically set aside.

Marriage in the play has two widely differing aspects. It is a sacred bond, upheld by religion and requiring to be sustained by mutual love and trust; and it is a business transaction, a practical means of forming advantageous social alliances. Leantio and Bianca marry for love, but they neglect the social conventions surrounding marriage. As a result, they are vulnerable to social pressures; and there is a strong implication that Leantio is blameworthy for having taken Bianca without her parents' consent. He himself sees his misfortune as a fitting punishment for this error:

> Here stands the poor thief now that stole the treasure
> And he's not thought on . . .
> Oh equal justice, thou hast met my sin
> With a full weight; I'm rightly now oppressed:
> All her friends' heavy hearts lie in my breast.
>
> (III.3.88–96)

At the other extreme, Isabella is being forced to marry a man she despises merely because he is wealthy and her father is intent on the material advantages to be gained by the match. We see the evils which flow from this loveless situation, in her reckless affair with Hippolito.

The institution of marriage is disgraced even further by the wedding of Bianca and the Duke. No amount of courtly sophistication can disguise the scandalousness of the ceremonies. The remarkable exchanges in Act IV, Scene 3, involving the Duke, Bianca and the Cardinal, appear to end in triumph for Bianca's clever reasoning; but the Cardinal sees clearly that her words point the way to dreadful retribution:

> Lust is bold
> And will have vengeance speak, ere't be controlled.
>
> (IV.3.71–2)

The more Bianca insists on the sanctity of marriage, the more she enlarges the terrible wrong against her first husband. Her dying words acknowledge her sin:

> Leantio, now I feel the breach of marriage
> At my heart-breaking.
>
> (V.2.210–11)

Dramatic techniques

Soliloquies

When a character expresses himself, not to other characters, but directly to the audience, our inclination is naturally to accept what he says as reliable information. He is not involved in deception, or seeking any advantage. He is explaining himself and giving his view of the situation he is in. Middleton uses this form of communication liberally in *Women Beware Women*. Leantio, for example, reveals his state of mind to us on almost every occasion. Furthermore, there is a great deal of confiding in the play, especially between Livia, Hippolito and Isabella. As a result (with the possible exception of Bianca) none of the characters is mysterious. Feelings, intentions and motives are always made plain, sometimes with great dramatic power. Leantio's reactions to Bianca's faithlessness in Act III, Scene 3 are especially moving. Livia is within hearing, but decides to leave him to himself for a while, until he overcomes his emotions:

> What is there good in woman to be loved
> When only that which makes her so has left her?
> I cannot love her now, but I must like
> Her sin, and my own shame too, and be guilty
> Of law's breach with her, and mine own abusing –
> All which were monstrous. Then my safest course,
> For health of mind and body, is to turn
> My heart, and hate her, most extremely hate her;
> I have no other way.
>
> (III.3.332–40)

Deliberations such as these hold some of the deepest interest in the play. There is a growing moral tension, as evil-doing gains ground, and we expect the final destruction; but, at the level of events, the plot is somewhat straightforwardly predictable and lacking in suspense. That difficulty is resolved by the dramatist by means of spectacle. The masque in the final scene provides the play with a vivid climax.

Irony

When Leantio is challenged to fight by Hippolito, he reflects bitterly on yet another turn in his fortunes:

> How close sticks envy to man's happiness!
> When I was poor, and little cared for life,
> I had no such means offered me to die;
> No man's wrath minded me.
>
> (IV.2.32–5)

He perceives the irony of his situation. Wealth and favour, which, since he lost Bianca, he has regarded as conditions of happiness, are now the cause of his downfall. The reversals of expectation which afflict Leantio in his marriage have already been noticed (see p.33). A further irony is that he should be killed by a man who is himself involved in an illicit love-affair, in order to protect Livia's 'honour'. The pretext for killing him is that he has made no attempt to conceal his affair with Livia. He has become 'an impudent daylight lecher' (IV.2.10). Having been hopelessly secretive about his wife, he is showy about his mistress.

Many of the parallels, juxtapositions and resemblances with which the play abounds are full of irony. A comparison between Leantio and the Ward is hard to resist. One is quick-witted and poor, the other is insensible and rich. One steals his wife away from her parents, the other obtains his by means of parental pressure. Both lose their wives to other men. The banqueting scene in Act III, Scene 3 brings them all together; and here another parallel is suggested, ironically, between Leantio's grief at Bianca's infidelity and Hippolito's vexation at Isabella's marriage to the Ward:

'Tis some man's luck to keep the joys he likes
Concealed for his own bosom, but my fortune
To set 'em out now, for another's liking . . .

(III.3.194–6)

One of the most impressive scenes in the play is Act IV, Scene 1, where Leantio, finely dressed at Livia's expense, comes to reproach Bianca with her newly acquired wealth. Both have sold their love, but Leantio is unable to see any similarity in their situations. He boasts of his new-found patronage without any sense of moral inconsistency.

The Duke's decision to marry Bianca plunges his court into the depths of cynicism and hypocrisy. No decency is possible; all virtue is reduced to a sham. There is scarcely anything to engage our sympathies, and we are able to take a fairly detached view of the counter-plotting. Each of the characters meets an appropriate fate. Livia, active in destroying two marriages, takes the part of Juno Pronuba, the marriage-goddess, and is herself destroyed; the wedding cup from which the Duke and Bianca drink has been poisoned by Bianca herself; Hippolito falls victim to the Cupid's arrows; and Guardiano is slain by his own stratagem.

Formal representation

Women Beware Women deals primarily with close personal relationships. Thus, the kinship of Livia and Hippolito is crucial in the play, and the violated marriage-bond between Leantio and Bianca is its deepest concern. Wider political and social matters are subordinate in interest to the progress and fate of individual characters, although the religious theme becomes more prominent latterly. For the most part, the action is presented in scenes of domestic, amorous or confidential intimacy; but on occasion Middleton adopts a more formal, emblematical method which shows personal concerns in a wider context and leads us to a more objective view of the characters.

The solemn procession of the chief dignitaries of Florence in Act I, Scene 3, emphasises the vast difference between the humble, secluded domestic setting in which Bianca finds herself and the great world into which she will be drawn. The splendour of the scene is part of her first impression of the Duke. The contrast between her husband and her future lover could hardly be greater.

The game of chess between Livia and Leantio's mother in Act II, Scene 2 provides an extraordinary commentary on the manner in which Bianca is misled and seduced:

> Here's a duke
> Will strike a sure stroke for the game anon –
> Your pawn cannot come back to relieve itself.
>
> (lines 300–2)

The image of Bianca's position being calculated against, its weaknesses exploited, herself exposed to danger and finally captured, is compelling. Her protestations of virtue have no more effect than the last, despairing, defensive moves in the game. We see now the inexorable consequences of her imprudent marriage, which cut her off from family and friends and brought her to a strange land. In Florence, her condition is nearly one of social isolation. Leantio's absence and Livia's and Guardiano's manoeuvring make her isolation complete, leaving her practically defenceless.

The banquet in Act III, Scene 3 brings all the main characters (except the Cardinal) on stage, and includes a dance by Hippolito and Isabella. Hippolito takes the Ward's place in the dance, as he has in sexual relations with Isabella; so that what should be an emblem of harmony between a young couple about to be married becomes a parody, a travesty of that meaning. Our sense of corruption which underlies this scene is further deepened.

The nuptial masque in Act V, Scene 2, ostensibly celebrating marital love and fidelity, is used as a vehicle for enmity and revenge. The splendid show which has been devised to flatter the liaison between Bianca and the Duke involves both them and the participants in destruction. Like the game of chess with its planned moves, it creates an objective as well as an emotional interest in the progress of evil. We are fascinated by the manner, while we are appalled by the deed. We are reminded that vice in the Duke's court has become habitual and systematised: that it proceeds not only from concupiscence, weakness and impulse, but also from design, intrigue and calculations of advantage.

Interpreting *Women Beware Women*

None of the characters in *Women Beware Women* keeps our sympathies for very long. We feel some concern for Leantio and Bianca as they embark improvidently on married life. Subsequently, Bianca's vulnerability, the Mother's bewilderment, Leantio's anguish, Isabella's distress, are all pitiable at first. But, in each case, our sympathetic feelings are soon banished. Bianca quickly becomes callous. The Mother disappears from view after Act III, Scene 3. Leantio becomes haughty after being taken up by Livia. His anger and bitterness are less impressive than his earlier show of grief, and his death is not profoundly moving. Given scope, a talented actress might make much of Isabella's perplexities; but it is her libidinous nature which makes the strongest impact. The Cardinal is a worthy but forbidding figure: his zeal is more in evidence than his humanity. There is no one in the play who involves our compassionate feelings to any great extent. We are estranged by the dismal operations of selfishness, greed and cunning; and because our emotional involvement with the characters is reduced, their significance in human terms is diminished for us. In Hippolito's phrase, they are 'brought to nothing'. The triviality of the final masque befits their deaths, because their lives have become narrow, futile and valueless.

Evil-doing arouses strong feelings of moral indignation, but these tend to become impersonal and generalised on account of our objective attitude towards the characters. We consider questions of right or wrong in the play with a certain amount of detachment, not confining our view to the implications for this character or that. An abstract and intellectual view of morality takes the place of emotional reactions. Other factors contribute to this attitude. The readiness of the characters to indulge in moral analysis has already been noted (p.41 above). Some of the moral distinctions which are offered, and some of the situations, are quite abstruse. We may well wonder why the Duke should scruple about an oath when he intends to have Leantio killed (IV.1.267–78), or how Livia can be righteous with Hippolito after he has performed the deed:

HIPPOLITO: Will you but entertain a noble patience,
Till you but hear the reason, worthy sister!
LIVIA: The reason! That's a jest Hell falls a-laughing at:
Is there a reason found for the destruction

Of our more lawful loves? And was there none
To kill the black lust twixt thy niece and thee,
That has kept close so long?

(IV.2.61–7)

Again, some aspects of Isabella's conduct are obscure. Her 'sin' is a complicated matter of deceiving and being deceived, of paternal authority, and consanguinity. Quite refined moral constructions are needed to deal with such intricacies. The Cardinal's fixed notions preserve the play from too much subtlety of moral rationalisation, perhaps; but they, too, arouse interest at the level of ideas. Like the Metaphysical poetry of the time, *Women Beware Women* deals with the passions in a complex, analytical way.

Here, three possible approaches to the play are suggested, under the headings of Time and personality, Public and private concerns, and Marriage.

Time and personality

The beginning of Act IV, Scene 1 is light in tone, a brief interval of geniality in the sombreness of the play. Bianca is engaged in frivolous conversation with two ladies. They compare the times on their watches, and this leads to witty remarks about their lovers. When the others have gone, Bianca's thoughts dwell on the subject of the alterations which time brings about. Her present situation seems strangely at odds with her upbringing. But her tranquillity is soon interrupted. Leantio enters, transformed in his outward appearance, but inwardly still in turmoil. He is intemperate and abusive, whereas Bianca is politely composed. She makes a point which challenges his dire seriousness:

BIANCA: I could ne'er see you in such good clothes
            In my time.
LEANTIO: In your time?
BIANCA: Sure I think, sir,
            We both thrive best asunder.

(lines 59–61)

She implies that times have changed, that there are new circumstances to which they should adapt, that they are not bound by their past. This is a provocative argument which could be considered in different ways: as a piece of conscienceless insouciance; as an appeal to standards of courtly sophistication, in keeping with the tone of the opening dialogue of this scene (and also with Middleton's source in Malespini); or simply as a practical proposition. Whatever our view, we will find a difficulty in condemning Bianca out of hand at this precise point. Her young personality is changing rapidly, before our eyes, as it were. New facets of her character are revealed to us continually. Here, in one scene, she displays in turn charm, reflectiveness, cool control, and menace. Each mood seems a new development, requiring another response from us. In her case, especially, we are obliged to attend to the sequence of things. We have to suspend definite moral judgements, because her personality is volatile. In doing so, we concede that time and psychological factors have a bearing on questions of good and evil. We interpret her actions in the context of immediate pressures and circumstances; in the light of subsequent conditions; and according to what we can perceive of her state of mind. It is a complex task of understanding, since judgements which seem imperative at one moment may have to be revised or queried later in the play.

Women Beware Women explores the hypothesis that time renews the personality and diminishes responsibility for past actions. Other characters besides Bianca are observed undergoing change, apparently drawing away from their former selves. Hippolito, Livia and the Duke are none of them young, but each falls in love infatuatedly, yielding entirely to a new passion. Livia experiences love, as she says, for the first time:

> Nor ever truly felt the power of love
> And pity to a man, till now I knew him.

(III.3.61–2)

Her devotion to Leantio overcomes her loyalty to Hippolito, with fateful consequences. The Duke is deeply affected by Bianca. Guardiano says he

> ne'er knew him
> So infinitely taken with a woman.

(II.2.13–14)

In the successive phases of his affair with Bianca, the Duke seeks to normalise each new situation, regardless of the wrong-doing which produced it. Having seduced her, he attempts to secure Leantio's acquiescence; when Leantio objects, he has him killed and, hoping to silence the Cardinal, forms the design of making Bianca his lawful wife. The culmination of this course of wilful obliviousness to past deeds is reached in Act IV, Scene III, where both defend themselves on the assumption that they can validate their conduct in the present:

> The path now
> I tread is honest, leads to lawful love,
> Which virtue in her strictness would not check.
> I vowed no more to keep a sensual woman:
> 'Tis done, I mean to make a lawful wife of her.

(IV.3.28–32)

Bianca's sophistry goes further: she claims to have undergone a spiritual conversion:

> If ev'ry woman
> That commits evil should be therefore kept
> Back in desires of goodness, how should virtue
> Be known and honoured?
>
> (IV.3.58–61)

Ironically, she achieves a happy equilibrium just before retribution overtakes them all:

> This is some antemasque belike, my lord,
> To entertain time. Now my peace is perfect,
> Let sports come on apace. Now is their time, my lord.
>
> (V.2.69–71)

'Now' is emphasised: the present moment, she imagines, makes all good.

One of the problems which *Women Beware Women* confronts us with is that evil is involved with the maturation of a young personality. Determination of guilt is a matter fraught with uncertainty, because we must 'allow' time. Here, the image of the game of chess comes again to mind: one move leads to another; each move is partly determined by the previous one, and partly determines the next; each piece is affected by the disposition of the rest. Everything is held in a sequence, within which it can be considered in isolation, but not judged in isolation. Actions (it is supposed) have a decisive, irrevocable quality. Bianca, as she takes the poison, echoes the Duke: 'Now do; 'tis done'. But, as the Cardinal insists, actions have deeper implications and lasting consequences, which must also be taken into account.

Public and private concerns

Leantio's first speech at the beginning of the play, after he has been warmly welcomed by his mother, is addressed not to her but to the audience:

> 'Las poor affectionate soul, how her joys speak to me!
> I have observed it often, and I know it is
> The fortune commonly of knavish children
> To have the loving'st mothers.
>
> (I.1.8–11)

The audience is immediately made aware of itself as a presence, a dimension of what is taking place. This awareness is kept up throughout. Soliloquies and asides in *Women Beware Women* have a special function. They are used by the characters to explain themselves, to the limits of their self-knowledge. Livia, Bianca, the Duke and Hippolito actually appear on occasion to be making excuses to the audience, as if hoping to find indulgence for their frailties. Thus Livia speaks, after she has promised to help Hippolito to obtain Isabella:

> I am the fondest where I once affect,
> The carefull'st of their healths, and of their ease forsooth,
> That I look still but slenderly to mine own.
>
> (II.1.65−7)

We are made to feel that we 'know' the characters in a way that we do not 'know', say, Hamlet or Ophelia. They engage our interest in what they are as much as in what happens to them or what they do.

Two effects of this condition of awareness are observable. One is that we can usually see through the elaborate deceptions and self-deceptions practised by the characters, and are able to test their understanding against our own. Accordingly, we are unimpressed when the Duke vows to 'Live like a hopeful bridegroom, chaste from flesh'; or when Hippolito makes a case for killing Leantio:

> There's no pity
> To be bestowed on an apparent sinner,
> An impudent daylight lecher.
>
> (IV.2.8−10)

When Isabella, Hippolito, Livia and Guardiano pretend to be reconciled in Act IV, Scene 2, we contemplate their feigning with ironic distaste, having no illusions about any of them:

ISABELLA: Well, I had a mother,
         I can dissemble too. [*To Livia*] What wrongs have slipped
         Through anger's ignorance, aunt, my heart forgives.
GUARDIANO: Why, this is tuneful now!
HIPPOLITO: And what I did, sister,
         Was all for honour's cause, which time to come
         Will approve to you.
LIVIA: Being awaked to goodness,
         I understand so much, sir, and praise now
         The fortune of your arm, and of your safety;
                    (lines 183−90)

It is as if rival gangsters should hold a press conference. To the audience, they are all, to use Hippolito's words, impudent, apparent sinners.

Another consequence is that our sense of the difference between

public and private, social and personal concerns is thoroughly exam-
ined. *Women Beware Women* mingles the two spheres, but it does not
confuse them. Throughout, the distinction between society and the
individual is carefully maintained, and we have to govern our response
accordingly. Since so much, even on the psychological level, is
revealed to us by way of direct information, we may be disposed to
apply, injudiciously, 'public' standards to 'private' preoccupations.
For example, in Act I, Scene 2, Livia delivers some practical, sensible
opinions about the injustice of forcing girls to marry against their
wishes (lines 29–45), and Isabella is eloquent on the same subject
shortly after:

> Oh the heartbreakings
> Of miserable maids, where love's enforced!
> The best condition is but bad enough:
> When women have their choices, commonly
> They do but buy their thraldoms, and bring great portions
> To men to keep 'em in subjection.
>
> (I.2.166–71)

These complaints have a conventional ring, and a measure of sociolog-
ical interest. To some extent, Isabella's affair with Hippolito is a reaction against the prospect of marrying the Ward, and can be seen as a
kind of protest. But Livia's fabricated story, which (as far as we can
tell) she certainly believes, releases her in her own mind from social
obligations: she conceives that she no longer has to obey her father, or
avoid Hippolito as a blood-relation. Her involvement with him is
therefore very much a matter of personal volition, of attraction and
appetite. In social terms, she transgresses only in point of infidelity to
her intended husband, and we may be exercised in our minds about her
blameworthiness in that regard. Indeed, we may, if we are curious,
reason that a divided response is appropriate: that we should consider
her actions in terms of social morality on the one hand, and of her psychological condition on the other.

A similar distinction arises crucially in the case of Bianca. In break-
ing her marriage, she abrogates a contract which society and the church
regard as of the first importance, and also violates the love and trust
which she shares with Leantio. It is the second which is problematical.
The clearest evidence we have of the depth of.the love between the two
is in Act III, Scene 3, where Leantio pours out his anguish:

> Canst thou forget
> The dear pains my love took? How it has watched
> Whole nights together, in all weathers for thee . . .
>
> (lines 252–4)

> What a happiness
> Had I been made of, had I never seen her;
> For nothing makes man's loss grievous to him
> But knowledge of the worth of what he loses.

> (lines 323–6)

He implies that their love was not primarily carnal, but had a spiritual quality:

> Those virtuous powers
> Which were chaste witnesses of both our troths
> Can witness she breaks first.

> (lines 340–2)

This is Leantio's testimony, at some distance from the courtship he describes, which precedes the action of the play. There is no declaration of love of this intensity by Bianca, and we have to deduce what we can about her feelings for him from what she says earlier in the play, while she is in his mother's house (see Part 4, p.60). She is the only character whose emotions, we may consider, we are told too little about. She remains enigmatic to the end. Dying, she remembers Leantio:

> Leantio, now I feel the breach of marriage
> At my heart-breaking.

> (V.2.210–11)

But then it appears that she wishes to unite herself with the Duke:

> Yet this my gladness is, that I remove,
> Tasting the same death in a cup of love.

> (V.2.220–1)

Our approach to Bianca determines the balance of our view of the whole play. Is *Women Beware Women* first and foremost a play about inner natures, about emotional, even spiritual, weakness and default; or is it mainly about human conduct in a society in which vice and corruption are dominant? An inward, psychological perspective and an outward, 'public' one are both available to us, and we must manage them as best we can. Attentive to one, we are liable to be surprised by the other; as where Bianca reveals her plan to kill the Cardinal during the festivities:

> For he that's most religious, holy friend,
> Does not at all hours think upon his end;
> He has his times of frailty, and his thoughts
> Their transportations too through flesh and blood . . .

> (V.2.24–7)

In her dying speech, she expresses the two kinds of awareness concisely:

> But my deformity in spirit's more foul –
> A blemished face best fits a leprous soul.
>
> (V.2.204–5)

Marriage

The *Table Talk* of the seventeenth-century scholar John Selden contains some severe opinions on marriage, including the following: 'Of all the actions of a man's life, his marriage does least concern other people, yet of all the actions of our life 'tis most meddled with by other people.' *Women Beware Women* takes a general view of marriage, without diminishing the importance of love and personal choice. Leantio and Bianca have married for love. They appear at first to have a secure emotional, if not financial, basis (although a contemporary audience would have detected too much of fleshly lust in Leantio's feelings: it was held that carnal passion should be moderated in marriage). Our sense of the need for love and compatibility is enlivened also by the forced match between Isabella and the Ward. The relationship of two people, however, is only one of the aspects of marriage which the play examines. Marriage receives ample consideration as a domestic arrangement, and as a social institution, involving parental control over person and property. It is also a religious sacrament. In the setting of Catholic Florence, the authority of the Church can be emphasised. Leantio relies upon a union 'sealed from heaven by marriage', rather than on one of the forms of betrothal then customary in England.

Women Beware Women shows so much infidelity, concupiscence, venality and hypocrisy that an attack on the credibility of honourable and loving relationships between the sexes might be supposed. We are shown the cynicism of a prearranged seduction:

BIANCA:	Oh my extremity!
	My lord, what seek you?
DUKE:	Love.
BIANCA:	'Tis gone already,
	I have a husband.
DUKE:	That's a single comfort;
	Take a friend to him.
BIANCA:	That's a double mischief,
	Or else there's no religion.
DUKE:	Do not tremble
	At fears of thine own making.

> (II.2.345–9)

We see cold-blooded, mercenary match-making by Guardiano:

> Tomorrow you join hands, and one ring ties you,
> And one bed holds you, if you like the choice.
> Her father and her friends are i' th' next room,
> And stay to see the contract ere they part.
> Therefore dispatch, good Ward, be sweet and short;
> Like her, or like her not, there's but two ways –
> And one your body, th'other your purse pays.
>
> (III.4.9–15)

None of the sexual relationships formed in the play is distinguished by higher feelings. Self-interest and the gratification of sensual appetite dominate in the liaisons between Isabella and Hippolito, the Duke and Bianca, Leantio and Livia. The first uses marriage as a screen for an illicit affair; the second breaks a marriage, and the third is an opportunistic combination. Lip-service to ideals by some of these characters only makes the example of their conduct worse. Bianca's declaration of wifely devotion (I.1.125–41), Livia's defence of the rights of women in Act I, Scene 2, and Isabella's conception of 'the most blest estate' (I.2.177–82) all lead to a deeper disillusionment.

And yet the play affirms marriage. Cynicism is not completely overwhelming. Two characters who do not succumb to the selfish worldliness which overtakes the rest make a strong impression on us. First, the Mother stands out as a representative of humble, domestic virtues which are not discredited because they can find no place in the world of the play. Her remonstrations in the quarrel in Act III, Scene 1 are hopelessly irrelevant, since Bianca is preparing to desert Leantio; but they move us the more for that:

> BIANCA: Here's a house
> For a young gentlewoman to be got with child in.
> MOTHER: Yes, simple though you make it, there has been three
> Got in a year in't, since you move me to't;
> And all as sweet-fac'd children, and as lovely
> As you'll be mother of. I will not spare you.
>
> (lines 29–34)

Later in the play, after the Mother has ceased to appear, the Cardinal's vigorous attacks on the Duke's scandalous conduct restore our confidence in the play's morality. He reproaches the Duke with two things, principally: the state of his soul, and the example which he, as an important personage, gives to others:

> Every offence draws his particular pain,
> But 'tis example proves the great man's bane:
> The sins of men lie like scattered parcels

Of an unperfect bill; but when such fall,
Then comes example, and that sums up all.

(IV.1.215–19)

In Act IV, Scene 3, he interrupts the proceedings with a powerful speech in defence of the sanctity of marriage. He refuses to compromise for the sake of appearances. In the presence of the entire court, he denounces 'religious honours done to sin':

Must marriage, that immaculate robe of honour,
That renders virtue glorious, fair, and fruitful
To her great master, be now made the garment
Of leprosy and foulness? Is this penitence
To sanctify hot lust?

(IV.3.14–18)

It is a critical question whether subsequent events resemble the divine vengeance which the Cardinal expects, or look to be no more than cross-purposes and scheming gone awry. Either way, the fatal consequences of sin are demonstrated.

The Duke's decision to make Bianca his wife, despicable though it is, serves to reinforce traditional attitudes to marriage. He, the ruler of the state, marries for what can be described as reasons of social respectability. The scandal of the affair is too great for it to continue in the same way. A sophisticated, courtly arrangement, whereby husband, wife and lover live on agreeable terms, as in Middleton's Italian source, is here seen to be out of the question. *Women Beware Women* reflects a thoroughly conventional, conservative view of marriage. Licentiousness is allowed no grace or charm, but is consistently shown to be selfish and brutal, Perhaps that is the function of the Ward. He lowers the tone so effectively with his crass, coarse wooing that no illusion of refined, attractive amorousness is possible.

Part 4

Hints for study

The characters

In the final scene of *Women Beware Women*, three of the characters reflect upon what has happened and draw a moral. Hippolito describes the consequences of lust and forgetfulness in lines 146–66; Bianca, in a dying speech (lines 210–15) refers to the 'breach of marriage', and also to the deadly snares that women set for women; and the Cardinal closes the play with an allusion to the evil example set by the Duke. It would be difficult to say which of these speeches best summarises the play's moral meaning. The emphasis in each is different, but each carries great conviction, and none seems to have greater validity than the others. This diversity of points of view is typical of the play, which keeps us aware of the different purposes of several characters. Indeed, it is not a simple matter to decide which is the main character. Livia is dominating, in one sense, but strong arguments could be advanced for Leantio, Bianca, even the Duke.

One of the ways in which our awareness is controlled can be seen in Act IV, Scene 1. Here, the characters are scathing about each other. There is much vilification and reproach. Leantio calls Bianca a 'whore' (line 61), the Duke a 'devil' (79). For Bianca, Leantio is a 'poor base upstart' (110). We learn from the Duke that Hippolito is quick-tempered, 'a blood soon stirred' (131); and he speaks of Livia as 'base' (138), and of Leantio as 'an impudent boaster' (150). These subjective views generally reveal as much about the characters who express them as about those they describe. The Duke is perceptive, but we cannot associate our own point of view with his. The Cardinal's expostulations against his sinfulness later in the scene are a good deal more authoritative.

When considering the characters, we should be receptive to the multiple, many-sided interest which the dramatist creates. Especially, we should avoid making simplified or exaggerated judgements. Thus, if we decide that Bianca behaves wickedly, we should not try to make the point by insisting that Leantio is a blameless victim. Livia could perhaps be described as a monster of depravity. Nevertheless, we should be attentive to her reasoning, her motives, and her strong attachments to Hippolito and Leantio. Also, since there is an enormous amount of duplicity in the play, we should be wary of regarding speeches in praise of virtue as evidence of latent goodness. Each speech has to be considered carefully in its context. As Leantio says:

> that soul's black indeed
> That cannot commend virtue; but who keeps it?
> (III.3.167–8)

Language and imagery

Women Beware Women has to be read with great care on account of the terseness of Middleton's style. Sometimes meaning is so compressed that it is difficult to follow the sequence of the thoughts. The syntax is frequently strained; and the imagery is often disjointed, at least on the surface. At the beginning of Act I, Scene 3, for example, Leantio, in the space of ten lines, compares himself first with idle gallants after a revels, and then with poor workmen after a holiday. It is a confusing juxtaposition of social opposites. For the gallants, the revels are a 'holiday' from their accustomed idleness. The reader has to exert some mental agility to assimilate the two comparisons, which together convey Leantio's indeterminate social status. He belongs to neither group, but sees himself as having something in common with both of them.

Again, Livia's description of Bianca's squeamishness at II.2.471 is not very easily grasped:

> Her tender modesty is sea-sick a little,
> Being not accustomed to the breaking billow
> Of woman's wavering faith, blown with temptations.

There is an inconsistency between 'tender modesty' and 'wavering faith' (the latter, at this point in the play, implies nothing less than infidelity), especially if we try to imagine one afloat upon the other. However, if we regularise the syntax at the beginning of the first line to 'She, being tenderly modest...,' some of the awkwardness is removed. With 'use' (line 470) Bianca's modesty will cease to be tender, and will come to resemble 'honour', in Livia's worldly sense (line 475). The adventurous voyage upon which she has embarked will expose her constantly to temptations and the hazards of 'wavering faith'. In the space of a few lines, Livia sums up the circumstantial and inward changes which affect Bianca at this crucial moment in her life.

Partly because no one character dominates, we cannot soon distinguish particular speeches as 'key passages', or take a narrow view of the play's 'central theme'. The Cardinal has great moral authority; but Bianca, Isabella and Hippolito deliver some quite profound reflections; and even Livia's worldly wisdom carries some weight. Nevertheless, *Women Beware Women* does achieve a coherence, a unified view.

Study of the language and imagery will reveal something of how this is managed. For example, 'wit', 'simple', 'honour', 'peace', 'strange' are frequently-recurring words, and it is instructive to examine the different contexts in which they are used. Images of light and dark form complex associations of virtue and moral blindness, concealment and notoriety. The decay or degeneracy of love is described in terms of disease. Material wealth and personal attachments are closely intertwined. Religious images occur throughout, contributing to the density of the play's meaning. The following brief list of illustrations could readily be expanded:

(*a*)   BIANCA: . . . Heaven send a quiet peace with this man's love.

(I.1.127)

BIANCA: I love peace, sir.
DUKE: And so do all that love.

(IV.1.125–6)

(*b*)   LEANTIO: . . . Why do I talk to thee of sense or virtue,
That art as dark as death? And as much madness
To set light before thee, as to lead blind folks
To see the monuments.

(IV.1.94–7)

DUKE: . . . One that does raise his glory from her shame,
And tells the midday sun what's done in darkness.

(IV.1.151–2)

BIANCA: . . . From a man that's blind
To take a burning taper, 'tis no wrong,
He never misses it; but to take light
From one that sees, that's injury and spite.

(IV.3.61–4)

(*c*)   BIANCA: . . . Yet since mine honour's leprous, why should I
Preserve that fair that caused leprosy?

(II.2.424–5)

LIVIA: . . . He's not wise
That love his pain or sickness, or grows fond
Of a disease, whose property is to vex him,
And spitefully drink his blood up.

(III.3.353–6)

(*d*)   LEANTIO: . . . Who could imagine now a gem were kept
Of that great value under this plain roof?

(I.1.171–2)

FABRITIO: She's a dear child to me.
DUKE: That must needs be; you say she is your daughter.

FABRITIO:	Nay, my good lord, dear to my purse I mean – Beside my person, I ne'er reckoned that. (III.3.106–7)

(e) LEANTIO: . . . When I behold a glorious dangerous strumpet,
Sparkling in beauty and destruction too,
Both at a twinkling, I do liken straight
Her beautified body to a goodly temple
That's built on vaults where carcases lie rotting.
(III.2.14–18)

CARDINAL: . . . this body,
Man's only privileged temple upon earth,
In which the guilty soul takes sanctuary.
(IV.3.42–4)

Study of selected passages

The following passages will repay close attention, and it will be helpful to memorise parts of them. Generally speaking, however, there is scarcely anything in *Women Beware Women* that can be considered properly in isolation. The context and the significance of each passage for the rest of the play are especially important.

(a) Act I, Scene 1, lines 12–38   Leantio's joy at having obtained Bianca

(Oh you . . . up withal)

(b) Act I, Scene 1, lines 125–41   Bianca's first speech
(Kind Mother . . . woman's joys)

(c) Act I, Scene 2, lines 159–82   Isabella's feelings about enforced marriage

(Marry a fool . . . human reason)

(d) Act II, Scene 2, lines 369–87   The Duke seduces Bianca
(But I . . . our fortunes)

(e) Act III, Scene 1, lines 42–60   Bianca's changed attitude
(Troth you . . . Mother)

(f) Act III, Scene 2, lines 190–214   Leantio's changed view of marriage

(Oh thou . . . is dead)

(g) Act III, Scene 3, lines 241–62   Leantio, deserted by Bianca, remembers their courtship

(Oh hast . . . together)

(h)	Act III, Scene 3, lines 320–48 (Is she . . . beggar)	Leantio agonises over his loss
(i)	Act IV, Scene 1, lines 23–40 (How strangely . . . think on't)	Bianca reflects on the upbringing of girls
(j)	Act IV, Scene 1, lines 190–227 ('Tis no wonder . . . hell)	The Cardinal remonstrates with the Duke
(k)	Act IV, Scene 2, lines 1–19 (The morning . . . preferment)	Hippolito's motives for killing Leantio
(l)	Act IV, Scene 3, lines 1–69 (Cease, cease . . . grace)	The Duke and Bianca dispute the Cardinal's objections to their marriage
(m)	Act V, Scene 2, lines 146–66 (Lust . . . torment)	Hippolito's dying speech
(n)	Act V, Scene 2, lines 192–225 (Accursed error . . . reign long)	Bianca dies; the Cardinal's speech closes the play

A possible approach

The following discussion of (b) above, Bianca's first speech, indicates a possible approach, but will not serve as an example in every case. In an examination which includes passages for close analysis, it is essential that the terms of the question are clearly understood and complied with.

CONTEXT:
Bianca has been present on stage from the beginning of the scene. She has waited quietly while Leantio greeted his mother, and may have heard parts of their conversation, despite Leantio's request to his mother to 'speak low' (line 71). After receiving a kind welcome, coupled with an apology for the 'wants' of the household, she speaks for the first time. She is newly married, in a new situation, in a strange land. She wishes to make a good impression, to be accepted by her mother-in-law, and to put her at her ease. There is a wide social gap to be overcome, and she tries to offer all the assurance that she can both to her new husband and to her mother-in-law that she will settle contentedly in her new home.

STYLE AND ORGANISATION:
She speaks gracefully and with composure. Indeed, her speech has the

air of a set piece, as if she has been preparing it for some time. Obviously she is concerned to say the right things, but she does so with a certain formality and an air of accomplishment. She conveys that she is perfectly happy, that she finds her fulfilment in Leantio's love, that she has no regrets about what she has left behind, and that her contentment will not be affected by hardship or the vagaries of fortune. But she expresses herself in a sophisticated way. When she says that she will be 'as rich as virtue can be poor', she is referring not to a necessary poverty but to a poverty that is voluntarily entered into, and she seems to be drawing attention to the sacrifices she has made, holding them up as proofs of her virtue and love. These sacrifices, which she declares she 'rejoices' in, are indeed impressive, as is the calmness with which she expects mixed fortunes. The images of 'guests of all sorts' and the adversities encountered in trade show that, despite her assertion at first that 'nothing can be wanting', she has no illusions about the difference between the 'fortunes' she has left and those she has found. The former were wealthy and assured, the latter are meagre and unpredictable. She ends her speech with a reference to Leantio's birth as the 'birth-day' of her joys, cleverly associating her love with the 'birth-joy' which the Mother remembers in her first greeting to Leantio (line 4). Perhaps she sees that she has impressed the Mother deeply, for she does not wait for a reply, but turns directly to Leantio, rounding off her speech with a coquettish appeal for proof of his love.

Most of the speech is governed by a condition placed near the beginning: 'Heaven send a quiet peace with this man's love . . .'. We may wonder: what if heaven does not? Peace matters to Bianca, as we see on other occasions in the play, and she is prepared to go to considerable lengths to secure it (see Act IV, Scene 1, when, having convinced the Duke that Leantio represents a danger to them both, she remarks demurely, 'I do love peace, sir.'). What does she mean by 'a quiet peace?' Will it be disturbed by the difficulties which she mentions after? Does it depend on her own virtue and fortitude, or upon what Providence sends in her way? There is a hint, perhaps, that she is stating her terms: that she expects the others to show her some special consideration, to ensure her peace.

DRAMATIC SIGNIFICANCE:

It may be that Bianca is saying what she thinks she *ought* to say, rather than expressing her true feelings. We can hardly imagine that she feels absolutely no regret, or that she is undismayed by the situation in which she finds herself. However, whatever view we take of her speech – whether we think it is romantic, quaint, naive or precocious – it is still the first testimony Bianca gives of her love for Leantio and her intention of living as his wife and sharing his fate. We know very little about the courtship and marriage. We receive this speech as a pledge, a commitment, and we recall it later in the play. Meanwhile, Leantio's attitude does not encourage a romantic view. His attention is divided between practical arrangements and the prospect of 'good sport' in his marriage bed (line 104). He is slightly patronising about his wife's intention

> To take out other works in a new sampler,
> And frame the fashion of an honest love.
>
> (lines 94–5)

Points to consider

The questions and topics listed here direct attention to aspects of each scene in turn. Some are quite difficult. They are intended to suggest ways of investigating the play, not in essays, but in reflection or brief discussion.

Act I, Scene 1

(a) Leantio refers to himself as 'knavish' (line 10). What evidence do you find in this scene to cast doubt on the goodness of his character?

(b) Domestic arrangements, practical matters, are the main concern in this scene. We are told very little about the courtship which led to the marriage. Are we reassured about the strength of the love between Leantio and Bianca?

Scene 2

(a) Is the dialogue between the Ward and Sordido mere meaningless diversion? How does it affect the tone of this scene?

(b) Examine the distinction between love and lust. Which thrives more, and why?

Scene 3

(a) How is Leantio's view of married love conditioned by his circumstances?

(b) 'Love that's wanton must be ruled awhile / By that that's careful' (lines 41–2). 'Good careful gentleman' (line 108). Is there anything in Leantio's situation which could have a bearing on the Duke's role in the affair?

Act II, Scene 1

(a) Is Livia believable in her soliloquy, lines 63–73?

(b) Secrecy and discretion are part of Livia's instructions to Isabella. Do you think this piece of advice has any influence on Isabella's behaviour?

Scene 2
(*a*) Does Guardiano, of all the characters, deserve the severest blame?
(*b*) Examine the arguments which the Duke uses, and comment on his powers of persuasion.

Act III, Scene 1
(*a*) The Mother is no match for Bianca in a quarrel. What could a cleverer disputant have replied to Bianca's peevish and unreasonable complaints?
(*b*) What comparisons could be drawn between Bianca and Isabella at this stage?

Scene 2
(*a*) BIANCA: How should the Duke know me? Can you guess, Mother?
       MOTHER: Not I with all my wits, we have kept house close (lines 129–30).
       Both women are lying. What view of the Mother have you formed by the end of this scene?
(*b*) Leantio is a pathetic figure. Does he seem here to be a tragic figure?

Scene 3
(*a*) Examine the theme of wealth in this scene.
(*b*) Leantio cannot comprehend the change that has taken place in Bianca. Can we imagine that we understand her better and can we accept the change in her?

Scene 4
(*a*) Is this scene intended to amuse or appal us?
(*b*) What is your view of Isabella?

Act IV, Scene 1
(*a*) In this scene of wickedness and reproach, are there any signs of goodness or of moral awareness to be found in Bianca, the Duke and Hippolito?
(*b*) As the two characters are never on the stage at the same time, it would be possible for the part of the Cardinal to be played by the actor who plays the Mother in earlier scenes. What effect might this doubling have?

Scene 2
(*a*) Isabella returns to a sense of virtue, but vows revenge. Is this consistent or credible?
(*b*) Why does Guardiano join forces with Livia?

Scene 3
(a) What is the significance in the play of the Cardinal's religious view of marriage?
(b) Examine Bianca's arguments to the Cardinal. Is there any truth in them?

Act V, Scenes 1 and 2
(a) What is the point of casting the Ward as Slander in the masque?
(b) Why is the Duke not given a dying speech?

Essay questions

1. 'Leantio's chief disadvantage is lack of common sense.' Do you agree?
2. 'We must always bear in mind that Bianca is very young.'
3. Compare and contrast Hippolito and Guardiano.
4. 'I'm cunning in all arts but my own love' (III.3.313). Consider this aspect of Livia's character.
5. 'As the play progresses, we come to regard evil less with horror than with contempt.'
6. Discuss the theme of duplicity.
7. What does the Ward contribute to the play?
8. 'The fourth and fifth acts do not have enough of the element of suspense.'
9. 'Lust and forgetfulness has been among us' (V.2.146). What does Hippolito mean by 'forgetfulness', and how is it manifested in the play?
10. Discuss the impact of the Cardinal on the play.

Part 5

Suggestions for further reading

Recommended texts

Women Beware Women, edited by Charles Barber, Fountainwell Drama Texts, Oliver & Boyd, Edinburgh, 1969.

Women Beware Women, edited by Roma Gill, The New Mermaid, Ernest Benn, London, 1968.

Women Beware Women, edited by J.R. Mulryne, The Revels Plays, Methuen, London, 1975. This is the edition used in the preparation of these Notes.

Women Beware Women, in *Jacobean and Caroline Tragedies*, edited by R.G. Lawrence, Everyman's Library, Dent, London, 1975.

Women Beware Women, in *The Selected Plays of Thomas Middleton*, edited by David L. Frost, Plays by Renaissance and Restoration Dramatists, Cambridge University Press, Cambridge, 1978.

Selected criticism

BARKER, R.H.: *Thomas Middleton*, Columbia University Press, New York; Oxford University Press, London, 1958.

ELIOT, T.S.: 'Thomas Middleton', in *Selected Essays: 1917–1932*, Faber & Faber, London, 1932.

FARR, DOROTHY M.: *Thomas Middleton and the Drama of Realism*, Oliver & Boyd, Edinburgh, 1973.

HEINEMANN, MARGOT: *Puritanism and Theatre: Thomas Middleton and Opposition Drama under the Early Stuarts*, Cambridge University Press, Cambridge 1980.

HOLMES, D.M.: *The Art of Thomas Middleton*, Clarendon Press, Oxford, 1970.

KNIGHTS, L.C.: *Drama and Society in the Age of Jonson*, Chatto & Windus, London, 1937.

SCHOENBAUM, S.: *Middleton's Tragedies*, Columbia University Press, New York, 1955.

The author of these notes

JOHN CONAGHAN was educated at University College, London. He taught for a year at the University of Ghana, and did postgraduate work at McMaster University, Ontario, before returning to London to do research. He was an assistant lecturer at the University of Strathclyde for two years, and since then has been a lecturer in English Studies at the University of Stirling. He has edited Etherege's *The Man of Mode*, in the Fountainwell Drama Series, and *Dryden: A Selection* (Methuen, 1981).

YORK NOTES

The first 200 titles